THE MISSION OF THE FOUR SOULS

THE MISSION OF THE FOLK-SOULS

in relation to
Teutonic Mythology

*Eleven lectures given in Christiania (Oslo)
between 7 and 17 June, 1910*

RUDOLF STEINER

RUDOLF STEINER PRESS

Translated by A.H. Parker

Rudolf Steiner Press
Hillside House, The Square
Forest Row, RH18 5ES

www.rudolfsteinerpress.com

Published by Rudolf Steiner Press 2005

First published in English in 1929. This reprint is a facsimile of the
second edition of 1970

Originally published in German under the title *Die Mission einzelner
Volksseelen im Zusammenhang mit der germanisch-nordischen Mythologie*
(volume 121 in the *Rudolf Steiner Gesamtausgabe* or Collected Works) by
Rudolf Steiner Verlag, Dornach. This translation is published by permission
of the Rudolf Steiner Nachlassverwaltung, Dornach

A catalogue record for this book is available from the British Library

ISBN 1 85584 146 0

Cover by Andrew Morgan Design
Printed and bound in Great Britain by Cromwell Press Limited,
Trowbridge, Wilts.

The following lectures were given by Rudolf Steiner to an audience familiar with the general background of his anthroposophical teachings. He constantly emphasized the distinction between his written works and reports of lectures which were given as oral communications and were not originally intended for print. It should also be remembered that certain premises were taken for granted when the words were spoken. "These premises," Rudolf Steiner writes in his autobiography, "include at the very least the anthroposophical knowledge of Man and of the Cosmos in its spiritual essence; also of what may be called 'anthroposophical history', told as an outcome of research into the spiritual world."

*   *   *

Readers will find it helpful to devote particular attention to the Preface written by Rudolf Steiner in 1918 as an Introduction to the "sketch of the psychology of the development of peoples" given eight years previously in the following lectures. That many of the intervening years were clouded by the tragedy of war demonstrates the relevance of such a theme not only when the lectures were given but again now, after many decades, when symptoms of disruption are so strongly in evidence in the world. It is surely high time for the spiritual significance of the missions of the Folk Souls and of the Time Spirit to become part of men's consciousness and made effective in the life of the peoples of the Earth.

CONTENTS

PREFACE
written in 1918 as an introduction to these lectures given in 1910.

In these lectures, which were given in Christiania (Oslo) in June 1910, I ventured to give a sketch of the psychology of the development of peoples. The lectures are based upon the teachings of Anthroposophy which can be found in my books *Theosophy, Occult Science—an Outline, Riddles of Man, Riddles of the Soul,** etc. I was able to build upon this foundation because my hearers were familiar with the scientific views which are presented in my publications. That is the external reason for the choice of my point of view; there is however a further reason, an inner reason. The orthodox study of anthropology, ethnology, or even history, cannot provide an adequate framework for a true psychology of the various folk characters. Neither the information provided by orthodox science, nor the study of anatomy and physiology suffice for an understanding of the psychic life of man. If we wish to understand the inner life of an individual we must study the soul as well as the body, and if we desire to gain real insight into national characteristics we must explore the psychic and spiritual element underlying them. This psychic and spiritual element, however, reflects not merely the activity of individual human souls working in concert, but has its origin in a higher order. The higher spiritual element is a province in which modern science is a total stranger. Before the bar of science it is paradoxical to speak of Folk Souls as real entities in the sense that we speak of the reality of thinking, feeling and willing in individual human beings; and it is equally paradoxical to relate the

*Riddles of Man is not yet (1970) published in English. A translation of a section of *Riddles of the Soul* is published with the main title of *The Case for Anthroposophy*, with an Introduction by Owen Barfield.

evolution of peoples on Earth to the forces of the heavenly bodies
in space. But the matter ceases to be paradoxical if we recall
that one does not look for the forces which determine the north-
south direction of a magnetic needle in the needle itself. One
attributes the deflection of the needle to the effect of the Earth's
magnetic field but looks to the Cosmos for the causes of this
deflection. Shall we not therefore have to seek the reasons for the
development of folk characters, folk migrations, etc. in the Cosmos outside the peoples themselves? Apart from the anthroposophical view which considers higher spiritual Beings to be a
reality, a totally new element is introduced into these lectures
which sees a higher spiritual reality behind the evolution of
peoples and seeks the forces which direct this evolution in this
spiritual reality. We then investigate the facts which are manifested in the life of the peoples and we find that these facts become
intelligible on this basis. The conditions in the life of the various
peoples, as well as their mutual relationships, can thus be clearly
understood, whereas without this basis there can be no *true*
understanding of this approach. Either one must seek a basis
for the psychology of peoples in a spiritual reality or one must
abandon such a psychology *in toto*.

I have not hesitated to use the traditional names of the early
centuries of Christianity to describe the higher spiritual Beings.
An Oriental would choose other names. Nevertheless, although
the use of this terminology may be regarded as rather unscientific
today, there seems to be no reason to fight shy of it. In the first
place, we thereby acknowledge the essentially Christian character
of our Western civilization, and secondly, if entirely new names
were chosen, or if an oriental terminology were adopted whose
real meaning could only be fully comprehended by one who is
spiritually at home in that civilization, we should be in danger of
misapprehension. It seems to me that whoever wishes to investigate these spiritual relationships, assuming he does not reject
our whole approach, will not object to names such as Angels,
Archangels, Thrones, etc. any more than physical science
objects to terms such as positive and negative electricity, mag-
netism, polarized light, etc.

Whoever relates the content of my earlier lectures to the

painful trials of mankind at the present time will find that what I then said throws a flood of light upon what is taking place now. (February 1918.) Were I to give these lectures now you could well imagine that in the light of the present world-situation these earlier investigations were a necessity. Thus for example on page 23 of the first lecture you will find the following passage: " . . . we have every reason, especially at the present time, to speak quite impartially about the mission of the individual Folk Souls. Just as it was justifiable to maintain complete silence about their mission hitherto, so it is in order today to begin to speak of this mission. This is particularly important because the destiny of mankind in the near future will bring men together in far greater measure than has hitherto been the case in order to fulfil a mission common to all mankind. But the members of the individual peoples will only be able to offer their proper, free and positive contributions if they have, above all, an understanding of their ethnic origin, an understanding for what we might call 'the self-knowledge of the folk'." No doubt the time has now come when the fate of humanity itself demonstrates the truth of this view.

Perhaps it is precisely the theme of the "Folk Souls" which shows how spiritual investigation which penetrates into the supersensible reality of existence provides at the same time a practical view of life which also throws light upon the most diverse problems of life.

This is not possible for a view of life which only uses such concepts as are valid in the sphere of natural science in order to describe the nature and development of peoples. This mechanistic-physical science has been highly successful in exploiting the mechanical, physical and chemical resources for the benefit of civilization; but in order to promote the spiritual life of mankind we need a science which is spiritually orientated. Such a science is the first demand of our age.

Berlin, 8th February, 1918   Rudolf Steiner

SYNOPSES

The purpose of the following synopses is to facilitate reference to the particular themes and subjects dealt with in the different lectures.

Lecture One

"Homelessness"—stage in spiritual development. The reality of Beings who cannot be apprehended through sense-perception, e.g. Folk Souls or the Spirits of Nations. These invisible Beings work through visible beings. The Spirit of the Swiss people. The anthroposophical view of man: physical body, etheric body, astral body and ego. In future time man will transmute these three members into Spirit Self (Manas), Life Spirit (Buddhi) and Spirit Man (Atma). The ego works through the three bodily members and develops in them the threefold soul: Sentient Soul, Intellectual Soul (Mind-Soul) and the Spiritual Soul (Consciousness-Soul). The task of certain epochs or nations is to develop one of these soul-members. The three former cosmic stages of man: Old Saturn (creation of rudiment of physical body), Old Sun (etheric body), Old Moon (astral body). The higher Beings—Angels, Archangels, Archai. Archai are guiding Spirits of civilization epochs, also called Time Spirits: they influence national character and temperament. Angels mediate between the Archangels and the single human being. In future man will be able to direct his body from outside. In order to know what a nation is we must understand the missions of these Beings.

Lecture Two

Climate, nature of the soil, plant-cover, etc. are the physical expression of a spiritual reality. A geographical region has not only a physical, but also a psychic and spiritual topography or aura. This aura is the sphere of activity of the Folk Spirit. Every people or nation has its particular etheric aura which is dependent upon the etheric emanations of the soil and the people domiciled in the particular area. This aura changes with the migrations of peoples.

Archangels cannot intervene where physical laws are operative. The Archangel sometimes withdraws: then the nation perishes. The etheric aura works into the etheric body of an individual and creates national temperament. It affects only the sanguine, choleric and phlegmatic temperaments, but not the melancholic.

The sequence of the Hierarchies above man. Beings who can remain behind as a deed of sacrifice are called abnormal Beings. Abnormal

Archangels responsible for the language of nations. Normal Archangels, abnormal Time Spirit and abnormal Archangel working in concert are responsible for the Old Indian temperament, sacred (holy) Sanscrit language and spiritual philosophy of ancient India. Spirits of Form create the present physical body of man which becomes the vehicle for the conscious ego. Backward Beings responsible for the present form of the brain. Normal Archai work in the thought life, give impulse to creative thought of the age, e.g. Galileo.

Emphasis upon Christ's relationship with the Beings of normal evolution. Before the coming of Christ men worshipped the Jehovah Being.

Lecture Three

Characterization of the inner life and consciousness of the Archangels, e.g. Folk Spirits. Archangels have three modifications of their etheric body which correspond to the three members of the human soul. Archangels do not share in the Sentient Soul and lower part of the Intellectual Soul, but in the realm of pure thought and moral feeling, i.e. in the Spiritual Soul and higher part of the Intellectual Soul. Influences of art and religion. The Archangel perceives rise and fall of peoples; incarnates in the springtime of a people and withdraws in its decline. Relation of Archai (Time Spirits,) Archangels (Folk Spirits) and Angels (guardians of the destiny of the individual). Sometimes normal Time Spirit intervenes in the field of the Archangel; a part of the nation is suddenly detached and forms a new nation, e.g. the Dutch detached from the Teutonic people, the Portuguese from the Spanish.

Interplay of abnormal Spirits of Movement with normal Spirits of Form creates the races of mankind. Difference between the concept of nation and that of race. Differentiation of mankind into races is the work of the abnormal Spirits of Form (or Movement). Racial differentiations enter more deeply into the physical.

Lecture Four

Important to understand how nations and folk communities arise out of races. Earth passed through three states or conditions before the present Earth condition. Ego-consciousness made possible by the Spirits of Form or Exusiai. The seven-year periods of man's development. Spirits of Form only interested in ego-development, i.e. man at age of twenty to twenty-one. Reason for man's dependence on Earth during the third of the seven-year periods.

Races began to be formed in early Atlantis. Racial types determined by locality of birth and transmitted by heredity. Diverse regions of Earth diversely receptive to cosmic influences. Importance of migrations. Centres of cosmic influence (diagram). Africa (here work forces which influence childhood), Asia (forces which influence adolescence), Europe (forces which influence maturity), North America (forces of decline). Today race is less predominant.

The civilization-epochs of post-Atlantis: India, Persia, Egypt-Chaldea, Greece, Rome and Europe of today. Westward movement brings decline of creative powers—an ageing process. The geographical areas narrowed from continents to islands and peninsulas. Need for rejuvenation from forces of the East, but man must find his spiritual resources within himself. Rosicrucianism implies evolution of all mankind. Evolution of races by evolution of nations. Plato's ancestry and race. Nation occupies an intermediate position between race and the individual.

Lecture Five

The lecture first enumerates the spiritual Hierarchies. Their working is manifested in the material surface of the Earth, e.g. the rocks of Norway. This is (outer) Maya. Two kinds of spiritual forces meet here—the forces of the Spirits of Will raying outward from within the Earth and the forces of the Spirits of Movement streaming in from the Universe. Formerly the Earth was in a semi-fluid state. The Alps and eminences of the Bohemian plateau resemble dammed up waves which have solidified. Spirits of Form brought the fluctuating forms to rest. The elements in which these Beings work: the Thrones in the Water-element, the Cherubim in the Air-element and the Seraphim in Fire. The Beings of the second Hierarchy work in the three Ethers; the third Hierarchy (Angels, Archangels and Archai) in the intermediate realm.

Each of the planetary epochs of the Earth has its special mission. Man owes his physical body and life of Will to Old Saturn, his etheric body and life of Feeling to Old Sun, astral body and life of Thought to Old Moon. The mission of the Earth epoch is to bring about the harmony of the three from within. The element of Love is added. Spirits of Form, creators of the Ego, are called Spirits of Love. The contributions of the different Spirits to Earth evolution. The need for man to raise his consciousness to higher planes.

The attendant Nature-spirits of the normal Beings of the highest Hierarchy: Undines, Sylphs and Salamanders.

Lecture Six

For a full understanding of cosmic evolution it is necessary to correlate the contents of the different lectures. The creation of races described in detail. The different races are the product of the co-operation between the seven Elohim and the abnormal Spirits of Movement. The abnormal Spirits are centred in the five planets and create the five root races: Mercury, the Negro race; Venus, the Malayan race; Mars, the

Mongolian race; Jupiter, the Caucasian race; Saturn, the Red Indians. This took place in Atlantis.

The planetary forces also work in man's organic system. Mars works in the blood. The abnormal Spirits of Movement in conjunction with the Elohim on the Sun and Jahve on the Moon create the Semitic race. Where they work in opposition to the Sun and Moon forces the Mongolian race is the outcome.

Venus and Jupiter work in the nervous system via the breathing and senses, producing respectively the Malayan racial type and the Caucasian or European racial type. The Greeks under the Jupiter influence; their idealization of the external world. Mercury and Saturn work in the glandular system. Mercury is connected with the growth forces of the body, hence Mercury creates the Negro racial type. Saturn ossifies the glandular system and creates the Red Indian; hence his bony features. Dialogue between a Red Indian chieftain and a European colonist. Red Indians preserved a clairvoyant memory of Atlantis before the separation of the races.

Lecture Seven

In post-Atlantean times the Archangels advance to the rank of Time Spirits or Archai. They are concerned with the events of late Atlantis and the transition to post-Atlantis. Distribution of races took place in early Atlantis; in late Atlantis a second migration took place. Nuclei of future peoples left behind in Asia, Africa, Europe. Archangels became their guiding Spirits. Culture-epochs named after those peoples whose Archangels became the leading Time Spirits. Time Spirit of the first post-Atlantean epoch was the ancient Indian Archangel. In the second epoch the Persian Archangel became the Time Spirit who inspired the original Zarathustra. In the Egypto-Chaldean epoch the Archangel of the Egyptian people became the ruling Time Spirit. In the third epoch an Archangel acted on behalf of Jehovah who had chosen the Semitic people as his own.

The two currents—pluralism and monism. Semitic race represent monotheism in religion and monism in philosophy, cf. Rabbinism. Other peoples represented polytheism and pluralism, cf. trinity of ancient India. Both aspects are necessary.

Two acts of renunciation on the part of Beings of the Hierarchies. The Greek Archangel remained as Time Spirit and becomes guiding Spirit of exoteric Christianity. Celtic Archangel remained as Archangel working among peoples of Western Europe, Southern Germany, Hungary and the Alpine countries. He was leader of esoteric Christianity. Mysteries of the Holy Grail, Rosicrucianism. Leading Time Spirit of fifth epoch chosen from among Archangels of the Germanic peoples. In Europe many Folk Souls acting independently: need to individualize peoples, hence late appearance of Time Spirit of Europe.

Time Spirit of present epoch subject to impulses of ancient Egypt—
hence materialism.

In remote past there existed, before the Celtic Archangel had established a new centre in the Castle of the Grail, above the Earth a spiritual
centre in the region of Detmold and Paderborn. According to legend
'Asgard' once situated here. From this centre the different Archangels
of Europe were sent on their different missions. In later years its spiritual
mission taken over by the Castle of the Grail. No other mythology gives
a clearer picture of evolution than Northern mythology. Germanic
mythology in its pictures is close to anthroposophical conception of
future evolution.

Lecture Eight

The characteristics of Teutonic mythology; contrast with Greek mythology. Superficiality of analogies of comparative religion. Relation
between mythology and successive civilization-epochs. In India high
spiritual level allied to dim ego-consciousness, cf. Vedas. Peoples of old
India closely associated with Spirits of Movement and Spirits of Wisdom.
Unable to apprehend Christ Impulse. Western peoples, especially the
Teutonic, awakened to the ego at elementary level of psychic development. Need to overcome old clairvoyance. Effect of migrations. Persians
looked to Spirits of Form, Chaldeans to Archai or Time Spirits, Greeks
and Romans to Archangels and Angels, normal and abnormal. Teutonic
peoples experienced transition from old vision to new, perceived Divine
Beings working directly upon their souls.

The two races of gods in Teutonic mythology; the Vanir and the
Aesir. Odin: resigned his evolution to give the gift of speech. His Initiation and the magic draught at the fountain of Mimir. Hönir gives
power of thought; Lodur: blood and pigmentation. Vili and Ve,
abnormal Archangels. Thor, son of Odin. Remained behind as an Angel;
transmits to the 'I' spiritual powers of the Archangel. Speech lives in
our breathing; ego incarnates in the blood: this is the hammer of Thor.
In macrocosm, winds and clouds related to breathing; in microcosm,
thunder and lightning to pulse-beat. Nordic man recognized Odin and
Thor in powers of nature. Niflheim and the twelve cranial nerves;
Muspelheim and the forces issuing from the human heart.

From Ginnungagap, the primeval abyss, a new Earth emerges after
the three Earth incarnations of Saturn, Sun and Moon. Imaginative
pictures of Teutonic mythology replaced by concepts in Anthroposophy.

Lecture Nine

Cognition of ego different from other forms of cognition. When the
ego knows itself subject and object of cognition are the same. Importance
of objective ego to Western peoples. Relation between ego and spiritual

2—MOFS * *

Beings—Lucifer and Ahriman. Old Testament knows only Lucifer, the serpent. Gospel writer (cf. St. Matthew) spoke of Satan, i.e. Ahriman. Old Indians looked up to the Devas; eschewed Asuras, beings of darkness. Persians fear Luciferic powers within man.

Loki and his three offspring: the Midgard Snake, Fenris Wolf and Hel. Loki is Lucifer. Consequences of Lucifer influence: selfishness in astral body (the Midgard Snake), falsehood in the etheric body (the Fenris Wolf), in physical body sickness and death (Hel).

Death of Baldur at hands of blind Hödur, an Ahrimanic figure. Extinction of old clairvoyance. Man now subject to Ahriman. Among Teutonic peoples clairvoyant experience did not perish completely, but unable to accept Christianity. Initiates taught them that attachment to physical plane and loss of vision only an intermediate time. Perception of spiritual world would return, but spiritual world would be changed. Lucifer would be overcome. This is the vision of Ragnarok. Connection between innate talents of Teutonic peoples and the vision of the future.

Lecture Ten

Subject of this lecture is the history of the European Folk Souls. Spiritual life of Europe a unity. Mission of Europe before and after Christ, to educate and develop the ego. Every single nation has its special contribution to make to this task. For development of the ego a mingling of races and nations necessary. Tacitus describes Germanic tribes as still immersed in Group-Soul. Celtic Folk Spirit helped to awaken ego out of group-soul life. The Druid priests and the Mysteries. Man had to become more self-sufficient; hence Mysteries gradually withdrew. The successive stages of post-Atlantean civilizations. Relation of culture-epochs to members of man's being summarized. Indians saw with forces of etheric body; in Persians, organ of perception was the astral body; in Egyptians and Chaldeans the Sentient Soul; in Greeks and Romans the Intellectual Soul. In the fifth epoch the forces of the ego are directed to the physical plane. Romans were founders of civil law and jurisprudence; Italy and Southern Spain subject to Sentient Soul, France to Intellectual Soul, Great Britain to Spiritual (or Consciousness-) Soul. In Britain union of ego and Spiritual Soul led to foundation of constitutional rights and Parliamentary Government. Outward orientation. Task of South Germanic peoples to prepare Spiritual Soul more inwardly. Hegel and Fichte: sublimation of clairvoyant insight of old Germanic peoples.

Polarity of India and China. Chinese civilization a static continuation of Atlantean wisdom. The Great Wall of China. Oceanus. The Gulf Stream encircling the old Atlantean continent. In the sixth culture-epoch Spirit Self will irradiate the Spiritual Soul. This civilization is being prepared by Slavonic peoples. Future potentialities of Russian soul in Solovieff. Solovieff perceives dual nature of Christ. His conception of a Christian Social State contrasted with Divine State of St. Augustine. To Russian people is given the seed of the sixth culture-epoch, but had to be nurtured by the Christian Time Spirit (who had been the Time Spirit of ancient Greece).

Lecture Eleven

Pictures or symbols of Teutonic mythology contain occult truths. Reference to *Occult Science—an Outline* which describes the descent of human souls from the planetary spheres in late Lemurian and Atlant-can times and their incarnation in human bodies. This event perceived clairvoyantly by those on Earth. The memory of this event survived amongst Southern Germanic peoples and was described by Tacitus in his *Germania*. Worship of Goddess Nerthus. Evolution on physical plane inspired by earlier stages of clairvoyance. Freyr, continuer of old clairvoyance. Riesenheim. Marriage of Freyr and Gerda. Symbols of Freyr's horse Bluthof and his magic ship. End of Kali Yuga in 1899 and the second coming of Christ. This will not be a physical manifestation, but will be etherically perceived—at first by a select few, then by increasing numbers of people. Need for objectivity: occult teaching accepts neither dogmas nor authorities. All teachings to be verified. Dangers of new materialism which looks for Christ's return in a physical body. False Messiahs, e.g. Sabbatai Zevi in the seventeenth century.

Ragnarok again. Picture of relics of old clairvoyance in Fenris Wolf. Forces of old Gods no longer avail. Danger of survival of old clairvoyance in future. Old clairvoyance must be transformed. The Christ in etheric form will drive out old, dark clairvoyant powers, i.e. Vidar will over-come the Fenris Wolf. Future mission of Teutonic Archangel. Import-ance of Slavonic peoples for spiritual development of all mankind. All nations to contribute to united progress of mankind. Christ Impulse overcomes separation: Christianity leads to ideal of the brotherhood of man.

LECTURE ONE

Angels, Folk Spirits, Time Spirits:
their part in the Evolution of Mankind.

It affords me great pleasure to speak at greater length for the third time to our friends in Norway and I should like to say briefly, in response to the cordial greetings of our friend Mr. Eriksen, that I reciprocate them in an equally cordial and heartfelt manner.

I hope that the course of lectures which I am about to undertake will contribute in some degree to the general understanding of Anthroposophy. In the course of these lectures I should like to draw your attention to the fact that they must of necessity incorporate much that touches upon the fundamental truths of Spiritual Science and, at the same time, something that, as yet, is rather remote from man's thinking today. I therefore beg especially those of our friends who are less familiar with the wider questions of Anthroposophy to bear in mind that we should not make progress in our field of investigation if, from time to time, we did not repeatedly take a great leap forward into those regions of spiritual knowledge which are really somewhat remote from the thinking, feeling and perception of man today.

From this point of view it will sometimes be necessary to ask you to accept what I shall have to say with a certain amount of good-will, since to provide the necessary evidence and proof for my statements in the forthcoming lectures would demand more time than I have at my disposal. We should not break new ground in this sphere if I did not appeal to a modicum of good-will in you and to your sympathetic spiritual understanding. Indeed the province we touch upon here is one which hitherto has been more or less eschewed particularly by occultists, mystics and theosophists, and has been eschewed for the very reason that greater objectivity is necessary if we are to accept the information I propose to offer without occasionally arousing a certain degree of opposition.

Perhaps the implications of this will be best understood if you recall that at a certain stage of mystic or occult development one is called a 'homeless man'. This is a technical expression. And if we wish to characterize without further ado—since we are not discussing the path of knowledge—what we understand by the term 'homeless man' we may briefly say that a 'homeless man' is one whose understanding and grasp of the great laws of humanity cannot be influenced by whatsoever a person acquires through association with his native country. Furthermore, a 'homeless man' is one who is able to identify himself with the great laws of human evolution without allowing the particular shades of feeling and sentiment associated with his native country to colour his outlook. It follows then that a certain degree of maturity in mystical and occult development demands an unprejudiced attitude towards our heritage that we justifiably consider to be an inestimable boon and which, on the other hand, in relation to the individual human life, we describe as the mission of the individual Folk Spirits who, by drawing upon the hidden roots and the spirit of the individual peoples make their individual concrete contributions to the collective mission of humanity.

We propose therefore to describe this heritage from which the 'homeless man' must liberate himself to some extent. Now the 'homeless men' of all times, from primeval ages down to our own day, have always known that if they were to describe in detail the state of homelessness they would meet with little understanding. In the first place the voice of prejudice would reproach them for having severed their connection with their native soil, for having sacrificed their heritage. This is not so, however. In reality, homelessness is, or may be, a détour, so that, once this sanctuary, the state of homelessness, has been reached, the 'homeless man' may rediscover the quintessence of the folk and achieve a harmonious relationship with the stable element in the evolution of mankind. From the outset it is necessary to draw attention to this. On the other hand, we have every reason, especially at the present time,

to speak quite impartially about the mission of the individual
Folk Souls. Just as it was justifiable to maintain complete silence
about their mission hitherto, so it is in order today to begin to
speak of this mission. It is particularly important because the
destiny of mankind in the near future will bring men together in
far greater measure than has hitherto been the case in order to
fulfil a mission common to all mankind. But the members of the
individual peoples will only be able to offer their proper, free and
positive contributions if they have, above all, an understanding
of their ethnic origin, an understanding for what we might call
"the self-knowledge of the folk". The injunction "Know thyself!"
played an important part in the Apollinian Mysteries of ancient
Greece. In the not too distant future the following injunction
will be addressed to the Folk Souls: "Know yourselves as Folk
Souls." This maxim will have a certain significance for the activity of mankind in the future.

Now in our age it is particularly difficult to admit the existence
of Beings who are inaccessible to sense-perception. Today,
however, we may be more prepared to acknowledge that certain
members of man's being are supersensible and invisible. The idea
that beings such as man, who at least in their external aspect can
be apprehended physically, may also have invisible, supersensible members will be more readily accepted by the modern
materialist outlook. But it is asking a great deal of our present age
to believe in the existence of beings who, from the ordinary
point of view, have no reality. For what is meant by the term
Folk Soul or Folk Spirit which one hears from time to time?
At best it is something that is acknowledged to be a common
characteristic peculiar to hundreds and millions of people
concentrated in a certain geographical area. It is difficult to
persuade the man of today that, in addition to the teeming
millions in this area, a living reality exists there, a reality that he
would find to be identical with the conception of the Folk Spirit
and which underlies this conception. If we were to ask—to take a
case that is non-controversial—what do we understand today
by the Swiss Folk Spirit, we would describe in abstract terms a
few characteristics peculiar to the people inhabiting the Swiss
regions of the Alps and Jura. It would be perfectly clear to us

that this description bears no relation to anything that might be known through external cognition. The first steps towards the understanding of this living reality is the frank admission that it is possible to envisage the existence of real Beings who are not immediately perceptible to the senses; that there exist amongst the beings perceptible to the senses other Beings invisibly at work, who express themselves through visible beings just as the human being expresses himself through his fingers and hands. We may therefore speak of a Swiss Folk Spirit in the same way as we speak of the Spirit of a man. We can just as clearly distinguish between the Spirit of man and his ten fingers which are organs of this Spirit as we can distinguish the Swiss Folk Spirit from the millions of people living in the mountains of Switzerland. The Folk Spirit is something quite different from the people, but nevertheless a spiritual Being, just as man himself is a spiritual being. The difference between man and the Folk Spirit is that man's external form is known through the medium of the senses. Whilst the human being is known through sense-perception, a Folk Spirit has no external manifestation; it is not something that can be known through sense-experience or sensory impressions and yet it is unmistakeably a real Being.

Today we shall endeavour as far as possible to form an idea of such a Being. How do we proceed in Spiritual Science if we wish to form an idea of a real Being? I propose to illustrate this by a characteristic example. First, we study the being of man. From the point of view of Anthroposophy we distinguish the physical body, etheric body, astral or sentient body and 'I' or ego which we look upon as the highest member. We know therefore that the man of the present day consists of these bodies. Now you already know that we look forward to an evolution of mankind in the future and that the ego works upon the three lower members of the human being, spiritualizes them and transmutes them from the present lower form into the higher form of the future. The ego will transmute the astral body into Manas or Spirit Self, so that it becomes something different from what it is today. In the same way, at a higher level, the ego will refashion and transmute the etheric or life-body into Life Spirit or Buddhi. Finally the highest achievement of man that we can envisage at present is the spiritualization of the physical body, the most intractible member of his being. When our present physical body, the densest and most material member, is transmitted into Atma or Spirit Man it will be the highest member of man's being. Thus we are familiar with three members of the human organism which were developed in past epochs, the organism in which we are at present incarnated and three others which the ego will fashion into something new in the future.

Between the initial development of the higher members in the past and their further development in the future there lies an intermediate stage. We know that we must think of the ego itself as inwardly organized. The ego works upon a kind of intermediate being. Therefore, between the astral body which man has inherited from the past and the Spirit Self or Manas which he will fashion out of the astral body in the distant future, there are the three preparatory members; the Sentient Soul, the lowest member in which the ego has already worked, the Intellectual or Mind-Soul and the Spiritual or Consciousness-Soul. But very little of Spirit Self or Manas that we are in process of developing is present in man today, at most only the first indications. On the other hand, man has laid the foundations of this future development by having learnt to control his three lower members to some extent. He learned to control the astral body by permeating it with his ego and forming the Sentient Soul within it. Just as the Sentient Soul stands in a certain relationship to the sentient body, so does the Intellectual Soul or Mind-Soul to the etheric body, so that the Intellectual or Mind-Soul is a feeble foreshadowing of what the Life Spirit or Buddhi will be—a feeble foreshadowing, it is true, but none the less a foreshadowing. And in the Spiritual Soul (or Consciousness-Soul) the 'I' has worked down into the physical body to a certain extent. Therefore the Spiritual Soul is a feeble foreshadowing of what will one day be Spirit Man or Atma. Thus, apart from the limited transformation of his astral body which he has already achieved as a first step towards the development of Spirit Self or Manas, we recognize in man today four different members. We can distinguish:

1. the physical body,

2. the etheric body,

3. the astral body,

4. the ego that works within them, and further as a foreshadowing of the higher members:

> the Sentient Soul,
> the Intellectual or Mind-Soul,
> the Spiritual Soul or Consciousness-Soul.

Such is man as we know him today; such is our understanding of
man at the present stage of his evolution. We clearly see the ego
fashioning the higher members after the Sentient, Intellectual and
Spiritual Souls have already prepared the ground. We see the ego
working with the forces of the Sentient, Intellectual and Spiritual
Souls upon the astral body, upon the embryo of Spirit Self. We
see man participating in this stage of his development.

Those of you—no doubt the majority of you—who have
concerned yourselves with researches into the Akashic Record,
with the evolution of man in the primeval past and the prospect
for the distant future, will know that man, such as I have portrayed him in the brief sketch I have given you, has evolved. We
can look into a distant past when man required long epochs of
time for his evolution in order to prepare the foundations, first
for his physical body, then for the etheric body and finally for the
astral body, and then to develop these three members further.
You will also be aware, no doubt, that man did not complete
the earlier evolution of his being, the evolution of his astral body,
for example, at a time when the Earth was in the same condition
as it is today, but that he developed his astral body in an earlier
Earth cycle, the Old Moon epoch. Just as we recognize that our
present life is the consequence of earlier incarnations, so too do we
realize that the Earth itself has known earlier incarnations.
The Sentient Soul and the Intellectual Soul were first created
during our present Earth epoch, the astral body during the epoch
of the Old Moon, the etheric body in a still earlier stage, that of
the Old Sun, and the physical body during ancient Saturn.
Thus we look back to three incarnations of the Earth and in each
of these incarnations we see one of the members which man

bears within him today implanted first as a seed and then perfected further.

In speaking of Old Saturn, Old Sun and Old Moon conditions another factor must be borne in mind. We human beings (on Earth) are now living through the stage of self-consciousness which other Beings underwent during the earlier stages of our Earth-evolution, the stages of Old Moon, Old Sun and Old Saturn. It is immaterial whether we adopt the terminology of the East or the more familiar terminology of the West in order to describe these Beings. Those Beings who underwent their human stage on Old Moon and who therefore are one stage above Man were called in Christian esoteric terminology, Angeloi or Angels. They are one stage higher than man because they completed their stage of human evolution one epoch earlier. Their mode of existence on the Old Moon differed from that of man on Earth today. They were Beings at the human stage, but were not incarnated in a physical body. Their stage of evolution corresponded to the human stage which man is experiencing today. In the same way we find Beings of a higher order who underwent their human stage on the Old Sun. These Beings are the Archangeloi or Archangels who are two stages beyond man and who underwent their human stage two epochs earlier. If we go still further back to the first incarnation of our Earth-existence, to Old Saturn, we find that those Beings whom we called the Spirits of Personality or Archai underwent their human stage on Old Saturn. If we take our starting-point from those Beings who were men in the primeval past, on Old Saturn, and follow the incarnations of the Earth down to our own time, we have a picture of the stages of evolution of the various Beings down to the present day. To summarize: the First Beginnings, the Archai, were men on Old Saturn, the Archangels or Archangeloi were men on Old Sun, the Angels or Angeloi were men on Old Moon and men are men on our Earth.

Since we know that we continue our evolution into the future and that we further develop our present astral body, etheric or life-body and our physical body, the question arises: is it not equally natural that the Beings who have already experienced the human stage have now reached the stage when they are transmuting their astral body into Spirit Self or Manas? Just as during the next incarnation of the Earth, the Jupiter stage, we shall complete the transmutation of our astral body into Spirit Self or Manas, so the Angeloi who underwent the human stage on Old Moon have completed the transmutation of their astral bodies into Spirit Self or Manas, or will do so during our Earth-evolution, a stage that we shall first have to undergo in the next incarnation of the Earth. If we look still further back to the Beings who underwent the human stage on Old Sun, we realize that they already experienced on Old Moon the stage we shall have to experience for the first time in the next incarnation of the Earth. They are performing the work which will be the prerogative of man when, in his ego, he transmutes his etheric or life-body into Life Spirit or Buddhi. These Archangels, therefore, are Beings who are two stages beyond man; they have reached the stage that will one day be ours when, from within our ego, we shall trans-form the life-body into Life Spirit or Buddhi. When we con-template these Beings, we recognize them as Beings who are two stages beyond ourselves, who foreshadow what we ourselves will experience in the future; they are Beings who are now working upon their etheric or life-body and are transmuting it into Life Spirit or Buddhi. In the same way we are aware of yet higher Beings, the Spirits of Personality (Archai). They are at a still higher stage than the Archangels, a stage which man will reach in a still more distant future when he will be able to transmute his physical body into Atma or Spirit Man.

As surely as man is at the present stage of development, so surely are these higher Beings at the respective stages of develop-ment which I have just characterized. We doubt their reality as little as we doubt their superiority to ourselves. Now this reality is not unrelated to our life on Earth; it penetrates into it and acts upon it. The question now is: what form does the activity of these higher Beings take? In order to understand this, we must bear in mind that from a spiritual aspect the activity of such Beings will be different from that of man today. Indeed there is a considerable difference between these Beings who are higher than man and those who are now only at the human stage. Strange as this may seem, it will become perfectly clear to you in the course of the following lectures. True spiritual investigation shows that man, such as we know him today, is, to a certain extent, at an intermediate stage of his existence. His ego will not always work upon his lower vehicles in the same way as it does today. The whole human entity at the present time is to some extent an interrelated whole and forms, as it were, an unbroken unity. This situation will be considerably modified in the future evolution of mankind. When ultimately man will have developed so far that he will be able to work upon his astral body in full consciousness and, by means of his ego, transmute his astral body into Spirit Self or Manas, then he will experience in full consciousness a condition akin to the unconscious or subconscious state of man during sleep.

Consider for a moment the condition of man in sleep. His astral body and ego relinquish his physical and etheric bodies which he leaves behind in the bed, and float outside them. Now imagine that in this condition man awakens to self-consciousness, that he is as fully conscious in his spiritual body as in his waking life. How remarkable would be man's impression of himself! At one moment he would feel: "Here am I; below me, perhaps some distance away, are lying my physical and etheric bodies which are part of me, whilst I with my other members am floating outside and above them." If, at the present time, man becomes conscious in his astral body, i.e. outside his physical and etheric bodies, then he is limited to the free and random movements of his astral body and can be active in the world independently of his physical body, activities which are denied to his physical and etheric bodies. In the distant future, however, he will be able to direct them from outside—for example, from a place in the north of Europe to some other place; he will be able to command their movements and direct them externally. That is not yet possible at present, but it will be a possibility when he has evolved from the stage of Earth-evolution to that of Jupiter, the next stage in the evolution of man. We shall then feel that we can direct ourselves from without. That is the essential step. And this implies a transformation of man's present condition. Here materialistic consciousness is at a loss. It is unable to realize that the spiritual activities now at work to some extent in the external world will also be active within the human being at some future time.

Such phenomena exist already and man could perceive them if only he would give heed to them. He would then see that there are certain entities, for example, who have developed prematurely. Just as man, if he waits for the appropriate moment, will attain the Jupiter state at the right time so that he will then be able to direct his physical and etheric bodies, so there are beings who in a certain respect have developed prematurely. Such prematurely developed beings are to be found amongst the birds, especially the migratory birds. Here we have an example of the group-soul to which the etheric body of each individual bird is related. Just as the group-soul directs the regular migrations of birds, so will man, after he has developed Spirit Self or Manas, command his physical and etheric bodies; he will control and direct them. He will do this in a still higher sense from without when he has so far perfected himself that he is still in the process of transmuting his etheric or life-body. The Beings who can already do this today are the Archangels or Archangeloi. They are Beings who can already do what man will be able to do some day, Beings who are able to compass what is called 'directing the physical and etheric bodies from without', but who are able at the same time to work upon their own etheric body.

Try to form an idea of Beings living and working as it were with their ego in the spiritual atmosphere of our Earth, whose ego has already transformed the astral body and who with their fully developed Spirit Self or Manas continue to work on our Earth and into human beings, transforming our etheric or life-body; Beings who are themselves at the stage of transmuting their etheric or life-body into Buddhi or Life Spirit. If you imagine such Beings who are at the Archangel stage among the spiritual Hierarchies, you will then have an idea of what are called the "Folk Spirits", the directing Folk Spirits of the Earth. The Folk Spirits belong to the rank of the Archangels or Archangeloi. We shall see how they, for their part, direct their own etheric or life-body, and how they thereby work down into mankind and thus draw mankind into the sphere of their own activity. If we survey the various peoples on Earth and select out individual examples, then we see in the life and activity of these peoples, in the characteristic attributes peculiar to these peoples, a reflection of what we regard as the mission of the Folk-Spirits.

When we recognize the mission of these Beings—for they are inspirers of the nations—we are then able to say what a nation really is. A nation is a homogeneous group of people directed by one of the Archangels. All that the individual members of a nation perform or undertake is inspired by them, i.e. the Archangels. Hence if we can conceive that these Folk Spirits, like human beings, betray individual differences, we shall have no difficulty in understanding that the individual peoples reflect the particular mission of their individual Archangels. If we have a clear mental picture of how in the history of the world nation succeeds nation, how peoples work side by side, we can then imagine, at least theoretically—and we shall have more and more concrete evidence in the following lectures—how all these changing circumstances are inspired by these spiritual Beings. But at the same time it will be clear to us that, in addition to this activity of successive peoples, something else takes place in human evolution. In the period of time which we reckon from the beginning of the great Atlantean catastrophe and which so completely changed the face of the Earth that the continent which lay between the Africa, America and Europe of today was submerged, one can distinguish the epochs of the post-Atlantean cultures—the old Indian, the Persian, the Egypto-Chaldean, the Graeco-Latin and our present culture which in the course of time will pass over into the sixth cultural epoch. We also realize that various inspirers of the peoples have successively been at work in these civilizations. We know that the Egypto-Chaldean civilization continued long after the Greek civilization had begun, and that this in its turn perished after the birth of the Roman civilization. We are in a position therefore to observe the co-existence and continuity of the peoples.

But in addition to the evolution of the peoples and all that is associated with their evolution, a progressive evolution of mankind takes place. Whether we consider one particular civilization to be superior to another is of no consequence. To express a preference for the old Indian culture is a matter of personal opinion. But he who is not swayed by personal opinions will be indifferent to value judgments. Human progress follows ineluctably upon the necessary course of events, although some may later regard this as a decline. When we compare the various periods, 5,000 B.C., 3,000 B.C. and A.D. 1,000 we are aware of the existence of something that transcends the Folk Spirits, something in which the several Folk Spirits participate. You can observe this at the present time. How is it that so many persons are able to sit together in this hall, people who have come here from many different countries and who understand each other or try to understand each other when they touch upon vital questions that have brought them together here? They come from the spheres of activity of widely different Folk Spirits and yet they have some common ground of understanding. In the same way various people were able to understand one another in Atlantean times because in every age there is something that transcends the Folk Soul, which can bring the various Folk Souls together, something that is more or less universally understood. This is the *Zeitgeist* or Time Spirit, the Spirit of the Age, to use an unfortunate term which is in common usage. Each epoch has its particular *Zeitgeist*; the *Zeitgeist* of the Greek epoch is different from that of our own age. Those who understand the Spirit today are drawn towards Spiritual Science. It is this Spirit which, reflecting the Spirit of the Age, transcends the individual Folk Souls. At the time when Christ Jesus appeared on Earth, His forerunner John the Baptist characterized the Spirit, which might be described as *Zeitgeist*, in these words: "Repent, change your mental attitude, for the kingdom of heaven is at hand."

Thus for every epoch we can discover the Spirit of the Age, which is something that permeates the activity of the Folk Spirits, an activity we have already described as the activity of the Archangels. To the materialist of today the Spirit of the Age is an abstraction, devoid of reality; still less would he be prepared to accept the Spirit of the Age as an authentic entity. Nevertheless the term 'Spirit of the Age' conceals the existence of a real Being, who is three stages above man. It conceals the identity of

the Beings, the Archai, who underwent their human stage on
Old Saturn and who at the present time are working from the
spiritual aura of the Earth at the transformation of the Earth and
are thus undergoing the last stage in the transformation of their
physical body into Spirit Man or Atma. We are here dealing
with exalted Beings and the contemplation of their attributes
might well overwhelm us. They are the Beings who might be
described as the inspirers—or if we choose to use the technical
expression of occultism—the "intuitors" of the Spirit or Spirits
of the Age. They work in such a way that they take over from
one another and mutually support each other. From epoch to
epoch they pass on their mission to their successor. The Spirit of
the Age who was active in the Greek epoch handed on his mission
to his successor, and so on. As we have already observed, there
are a number of such Time Spirits, of such Spirits of Personality
who work as Spirits of the Age. These Spirits of Personality,
these inspirers of the Spirit of the Age, are of a higher order than
the Folk Spirits. In every epoch one of these Spirits of Personality
is predominant and sets his seal upon the whole epoch, assigns
to the Folk Spirits their specific tasks, so that the whole spirit of
the epoch is determined by the special or individual characteristics of the Folk Spirit. Then, in the following epoch, another
Spirit of Personality, another of the Archai, takes over.

After a certain number of epochs have elapsed, a Spirit of the
Age has evolved further. We must picture this in the following
way: when we die, having completed our present stage of
evolution, our personality transmits the achievements of this
Earth-life to the next Earth-life. The same holds good for the
Spirits of the Age. In each Age we have one such Spirit of the
Age, and at the end of the epoch he hands over to his successor,
who, in his turn, hands over to his successor, and so on. The
earlier Spirits, meanwhile, continue their own development.
Then the original Spirit takes over again, so that in a later epoch,
whilst the others are proceeding with their own evolution, he
takes over again and infuses intuitively into mankind what he
himself has acquired for his higher mission, for the benefit of the
more developed humanity. We look up to these Spirits of Personality, to these Beings who may be characterized by the somewhat
3—MOFS * *

colourless term 'Spirit of the Age'. Now we human beings pass from incarnation to incarnation; but we know for certain that, whilst we ourselves progress from epoch to epoch, when we look into the future, we see ever different Spirits of the Age determining events on Earth. But our Spirit of the Age will return too and we shall meet him once again. Because a characteristic feature of these Spirits of Personality is to perform cyclic revolutions and return to their starting-point, they are therefore called "Spirits of Cyclic Periods". (We shall justify the use of this expression by giving further details later.) These higher Spiritual Beings then who issue their commands to the Folk Spirits are also called Spirits of Cyclic Periods. We are here referring to those cyclic periods which man himself has to go through when from epoch to epoch he returns to earlier conditions and repeats them in a higher form. Now this repetition of the characteristics of earlier forms may surprise you. If you examine carefully the stages of man's evolution on Earth in the light of Spiritual Science, you will find that these occurrences recur in many different forms. Thus the seven consecutive epochs following upon the Atlantean catastrophe which we call the post-Atlantean culture-epochs, are a repetition. The Graeco-Latin epoch marks the turning-point in our cycle and will not therefore be repeated. This stage is followed by a repetition of the Egypto-Chaldean epoch in our own age. This will be followed by a repetition of the Persian epoch, but in a somewhat different form. Then will follow the seventh epoch which will be a repetition of the ancient Indian civilization, the epoch of the Holy Rishis, so that in this coming epoch certain aptitudes which had been implanted in ancient India will reappear in a new form. The direction of these occurrences devolves upon the Spirits of the Age.

In order that, distributed amongst the various peoples of the Earth, the progressive development of successive epochs may be realized, in order that the widely differing ethnic types may be moulded by a particular geographical area or community of language, in order that a particular form-language, architecture, art or science may flourish and their various metamorphoses receive all that the Spirit of the Age can pour into mankind—for this we need the Folk Spirits, who, in the hierarchy of higher Beings, belong to the Archangels.

Now we require yet another intermediary agent between the higher missions of the Folk Spirits and those beings here on Earth who are to be inspired by them. You will readily perceive at least theoretically at first, that the mediator between the two different kinds of Spirits is the Hierarchy of the Angels. They are the intermediaries between the single human being and the Archangel of the folk. In order that the individual may receive into himself that which the Folk Spirit has to pour into the whole people, in order that the single human being may be instrumental in fulfilling the mission of his people, this intermediary agent between the human being and the Archangel of his people is indispensable.

Thus we have looked up to the Beings who attained their human stage three stages above man and have noted how they placed themselves consciously at the service of mankind and influenced our Earth-evolution. In the next lecture we propose to show how far the activity of the Archangels working down from above, from within their Ego which has already developed Manas or Spirit Self and is perfecting the etheric or life-body of man, is expressed in the achievements, attributes and character of a people.

Man is directly associated with the work of the higher Beings, for, as a member of a nation, he is an integral part of it. It is true that man is, in the first place, an individual, a creation of his Ego-being; but he is not only an individual, he is also a member of a particular people, something over which, as an individual, he has no control. As a member of a particular people the individual has no choice but to speak the language of his people. He does not acquire this by his own efforts, it does not stem from his individual initiative, it is the legacy of his inheritance. Individual human progress is something totally different. As we watch the life and activity of the Folk Souls, we must bear in mind what is involved in the progress of man and what is demanded of him in order to achieve it. We shall see what determines not only his own particular development but also the development of wholly different Beings.

Thus we see how man is integrated into the ranks of the Hierarchies, how, from age to age, from epoch to epoch, Beings whom we already know from another aspect, cooperate in his evolution, And we have seen how opportunities are provided for these Beings to express themselves in a variety of ways peculiar to themselves and that what they have to offer can be imparted to man.

The guiding principles of the several epochs are determined by the Time Spirits (*Zeitgeister*). The single folk-individualities are responsible for disseminating the Spirit of the Age over the whole Earth. Whilst the Time Spirits inspire the Folk Spirits, the Angels act as mediators between the Folk Spirit and the single human beings, so that these individuals may fulfil the mission of the Folk Spirits.

One of the purposes of these lectures will be to show how this wonderful pattern reveals the working of the various folk-individualities, past and present. In the next lecture we shall begin to throw light upon how this pattern is woven which we have indicated only sketchily today, that spiritual pattern which represents our immediate destiny in the world.

LECTURE TWO

Normal and abnormal Archangels and Time Spirits.
The Spirits of Language and of Modes of Thought.

I stated yesterday that those Beings who are to be considered as Folk Spirits have reached a stage of development when they work from within the 'I' upon their etheric or life-body, when they fashion this body from out of the inmost depths of the soul.

Now it will be said, of course, that the work upon the etheric body is not immediately perceptible to the senses or to external observation but only to clairvoyant consciousness, and this must be admitted. None the less, if the activity of these Beings, of these Folk Spirits, invades the life of man, then there must be on the other hand some visible indication, some tangible evidence, some kind of impression or reflection of this work of the Folk Spirits or Archangelic Beings, in proof of this. Furthermore these Beings must also possess in a certain sense a physical body. They must be able to express their corporeality in some form or other. And these Beings whose activity is expressed in this physical form must give some indication of their presence in the world of man, for in the final analysis the human body must be associated with the work of these spiritual Beings.

Let us begin with the etheric body of these Beings and their work in the transformation of this body. Here we must first of all refer to the investigations of clairvoyant consciousness. Where does clairvoyant research find evidence for the existence of the etheric body of these Archangelic Beings? And how are we to understand this work? You all know that the surface of the Earth shows different configurations and that the different regions of the Earth provide widely differing conditions for the unfolding of attributes peculiar to the various peoples. The materialist believes that climate, vegetation, or perhaps water availability and other factors determine the distinctive features or characteristics of a particular people. That such is the outlook of the materialist is not surprising, for his consciousness is limited to the phenomenal world. Clairvoyant consciousness presents a different picture. Whoever is endowed with clairvoyant consciousness and visits the various countries is aware that his familiarity with the particular kind of vegetation, with the characteristic configuration of the rocks, does not exhaust his knowledge of that country or provide a complete picture of a particular geographical area. To speak of a particular aroma and aura associated with a certain region is, in the eyes of the materialist, to deal in unrealities. To clairvoyant consciousness there extends over every region of the Earth a peculiar spiritual cloudlike formation that we call the etheric aura of that particular region. This etheric aura varies according to the landscape: in Switzerland it is different from Italy and again different in Norway, Denmark or Germany. Just as every man has his own etheric body, so a kind of etheric aura hovers above every region of the Earth's surface.

This etheric aura differs considerably from other etheric auras, from that of man, for example. The etheric aura of the human being is part of him as long as he lives. It is united to his physical body and only undergoes modification in so far as man progressively develops during his lifetime and lifts himself to a higher moral and intellectual plane. Then we are always conscious that this etheric aura begins to be inwardly transformed, develops a certain inner light, a luminous quality. The etheric auras that can be perceived over the various countries are of a different nature. Admittedly they preserve a fundamental tone or quality which persists over long periods of time. But, at the same time, these etheric auras are prone to rapid changes, and in this respect they differ from the human auras which change slowly and gradually, and only from within. These auras extending over the various countries change in the course of human evolution when a people migrates and occupies new territory. The strange feature is that the etheric aura over a certain region depends in fact not only upon the etheric emanations from the soil, but also upon the people which was last domiciled there.

Those, therefore, who wish to follow how the destinies of our
human race are shaped on Earth, endeavour to follow the interpenetration of this aspect of the etheric auras which is peculiar to
the different geographical regions. The various etheric auras of
Europe underwent considerable change at the time of the
migrations of the peoples. Thus the etheric aura of a particular
region is subject to change, to sudden transformations which may
even have their source in external factors to some extent. Every
one of these etheric auras is, in a certain respect, a fusion of the
emanations from the soil and the inheritance of the migrations of
the peoples. When we observe this aura we must clearly understand that the saying, everything in the external world apprehended by the senses is only maya or illusion, which is so freely
quoted by Theosophists is seldom grasped in its fullest implications. Though often repeated, its implications are largely
ignored, and it rarely leads to a change of attitude to life. It
becomes virtually an empty phrase; in face of the stern realities
of life it is forgotten and people cling to their old materialistic
outlook. The green vegetation, the peculiar configuration of the
landscape which we see around us is, in reality, only maya or
illusion; it is a precipitation, as it were, of the active principle
in the etheric forces. Indeed only that aspect of the external
world is dependent upon this etheric aura, upon which this aura,
i.e. a living, organizing principle, can exert an influence. The
Archangels who embody the spiritual laws cannot intervene in
the physical laws. Where, therefore, only physical laws are operative, as in the configuration of mountain ranges, in the contours
of the landscape and so on, in all cases where physical conditions
determine the great changes in a people, the influence of the
Archangels cannot take effect. They are not sufficiently advanced
in their evolution to be able to intervene in purely physical
conditions. Because they are unable to do this, because they are
not free agents, they are compelled at certain times to wander
over the surface of the Earth, They incarnate somewhat after the
fashion of a physical incarnation, in that which is represented by
the configuration of the landscape, in that which is subject to
physical laws. The etheric body of the people cannot as yet enter
into this domain, cannot, as yet, penetrate into it and organize

it. Therefore a suitable territory is selected and from this union of the etheric body now permeated with spiritual soul-forces, and the geographical area, is born that charm or fascination which a people radiates, which is dimly sensed by one who is not clairvoyant, but which a clairvoyant who sees into the secret hearts and minds of the people is able to discern.

Now how does the activity of the Archangels, the Folk Souls, work into the etheric aura that extends over a country? What is the function of the Archangel, how does he work into the people who inhabit this country and live within this aura of the Folk Spirit? This influence expresses itself in three ways. The etheric aura of the people interpenetrates, permeates man; it affects three aspects of his being. The interplay of these three aspects creates the peculiar characteristic of the person who lives in this etheric aura of the people. This etheric aura acts upon the three temperaments, the choleric, phlegmatic and sanguinic temperaments, which are themselves rooted in his affective life, but not upon the so-called melancholic temperament. In general, therefore, the potent influence of the etheric aura of a people streams into these three temperaments. In the single individual these three temperaments may be variously commingled and interact in a wide variety of ways. There are infinite possibilities of interaction, as when one temperament influences another or dominates it, and so on. Here lies the source of the multiplicity of types we meet with in Russia, Norway and Germany. The national characteristics of an individual are determined by that which works into the temperaments. The difference between the several individuals depends entirely upon the extent to which the three temperaments are commingled. National temperaments, therefore, vary in accordance with the extent of the interpenetration of the folk-aura.

Thus the Folk Spirits are active everywhere. They follow, however, the path peculiar to them. The fact that they work into the temperaments is not vital for their own development; they only do so because they are involved in the interplay of cosmic and terrestrial forces. It is a volitional act, a necessary part of their mission. At the same time their own ego-development must be taken into account. They themselves must further their evolution, move across the face of the Earth and incarnate in a particular region. This is central to their mission; their influence upon the temperaments of men is of secondary importance. Naturally, man himself also benefits through their work; it reacts upon him. And equally, the activity of man reacts upon the Folk Spirits. We shall discuss later the significance of the individual human beings for the Folk Spirit. This is important. But it is essential that we should be able to follow the progress of one of these Folk Spirits and see how he incarnates on Earth, lives again for a time in the spiritual world and then incarnates again elsewhere. When we observe these recurrent changes we are still only observing the ego-interests of these Beings. Picture to yourselves quite realistically the etheric body of the human being embedded in the etheric body of the people; then picture the interaction of the human etheric body and the etheric body of the people, and think too of how the latter is reflected in the temperaments of the people, in the mingling of temperaments in the single individuals. Therein lies the secret of how the Folk Spirit or Nation Spirit reveals his character within a particular people. Having said this, we have, in effect, described the full scope of the most important work of the true Archangels or Folk Spirits.

We should by no means have exhausted the characteristics of a people if we were to take into consideration only the character of an individual member of this people. This is the function of the Archangelic Beings, who are the real Spirits of the indigenous groups of the same language-stock.

Now, as you can readily imagine, this does not complete the picture of a people, for if the Archangel, the guiding Folk Spirit, did not contact other Beings on the same territory and did not work in conjunction with them in the etheric body of man, many of the characteristics of a people would not originate at all. Man is the stage upon which the Archangels meet with yet other Beings who cooperate with the Archangels and, so to speak, work in conjunction with them. From this cooperative endeavour something totally different emerges.

When, with clairvoyant consciousness, we study the different peoples, we find, strange to relate, besides the Archangelic Beings already described, other mysterious Beings who are related to the Archangels in certain respects, but who are otherwise totally different from them, in that they are more potent Beings than the Archangels themselves. In this weaving into the temperaments the Folk Spirit works in an extremely subtle and intimate way upon the individual human soul. But there are other Beings who exercise a much more potent influence. From our general knowledge of the Hierarchies we must be quite clear about these Beings; we shall then be able to name these other Beings who are perceived by clairvoyant consciousness. You must think of the sequence of the Hierarchies of Spirits in the following way:

1. Man
2. Angels
3. Archangels
4. First Beginnings, Archai or Spirits of Personality
5. Powers (Exusiai) or Spirits of Form

There are yet other Spirits of a higher order who do not concern us today.

If you recall what we spoke of yesterday—and you will find a detailed description in the information contained in my books *Cosmic Memory** and *Occult Science—an Outline,* you will know that it was the Archangels who underwent their human stage on Old Sun. At that time those Beings whom we call Spirits of Form or Powers, who are now two stages higher than the Archangels, were at the Archangel stage; they were Beings such as the Folk Spirits we have described today. That was their normal stage of evolution.

Now there is a strange mystery attaching to evolution—the law of deferred development. In accordance with this law certain Beings remain behind at each stage of evolution, so that in the succeeding stage they have not reached their normal rank. They retain the characteristics which belong to earlier stages. Throughout the evolution of mankind there have always been Beings who

*Original title: *Aus der Akasha Chronik.* Published with the title of *Cosmic Memory* by Rudolf Steiner Publications, Inc., New York. (Obtainable from Rudolf Steiner Press, London. See the list of literature at the end of this volume.)

remained behind and amongst them are also certain Spirits of Form or Powers. Their deferred development took a very singular form. Whilst they are Spirits of Form or Powers in terms of certain attributes, and by virtue of certain attributes are able to exercise the powers that belong at the present time solely to the Spirits of Form who have bestowed the ego upon man at the Earth-stage, they cannot, as yet, realize this completely because they do not possess the necessary attributes. They have remained behind, with the result that they did not undergo their Archangelic stage on the Old Sun, but are now experiencing it in the Earth-stage. Hence they are Beings who are now at the stage of the Folk Spirits, but endowed with quite different attributes. Whilst the Folk Spirits work in a subtle way into the life of man because they are two stages above him and are consequently still related to him, these Spirits of Form are four stages above the human stage. They possess, therefore, a vast array of potent forces which would not be suitable for working so intimately into man. They would act more vigorously and would have no other sphere for their activity than that in which the normal Folk Spirits work.

The difficulty is that one must first learn to discriminate in the spiritual world. Those who imagine that a few ideas suffice for the understanding of the higher worlds are very much mistaken. With a few superficial ideas they would certainly contact the Archangels. But one must distinguish between the Archangels who have reached the Archangel stage in the normal way and those who ought to have reached that stage during the Old Sun condition of the Earth. Thus, other Beings are at work in the same domain as the Folk Spirits or Archangels, Beings who stand at the same level as the Archangels, but are endowed with very different, with more robust attributes such as are possessed by the other Spirits of Form and who are able therefore to penetrate deeply into human nature. In what respects has man been influenced by the Spirits of Form during his Earth existence? He could not have developed ego-consciousness if the Spirits of Form had not given the brain its present form. Beings such as these are able to work even into the configuration of the human form although they are only at the stage of the Archangels. They compete with the Folk Spirits in the domain where the Folk Spirits are active.

The first and major effect of this contact between these Spirits with their different approaches is the birth of language which could not arise without the fully developed form and structure of the human body. In the structure of man we see the activity of these other Folk Spirits who are associated with the forces of Nature and with man. We must not ascribe the birth of language solely to these Beings who subtly work into the folk temperament and who, as Beings two stages above man, imprint their formal configuration upon a people. The Beings who are responsible for language are Beings of great creative energy for they are in reality '*Powers*', i.e. Spirits of Form. They exercise effective influence upon the Earth because thay have remained on Earth, whereas their colleagues, the normal Spirits of Form, work in the 'I', work from the Sun into the cosmic spaces. Before the advent of Christ Jesus men worshipped Jahve, or the Jehovah Being; thereafter they worshipped the Being of Christ as the One who shed His Spirit upon them from the Cosmos. As to the Spirits of language, we must say that man cherishes precisely that aspect of language which has remained on Earth. We must learn to accustom ourselves to new points of view. Man is in the habit of projecting his own ideas into the universe. He would be wrong to regard the sacrifice these higher Beings have made in their evolution after the fashion of a schoolgirl who has failed to gain promotion. They do not remain behind because they have neglected their studies, but from motives of higher wisdom which is omnipresent in the world. If certain Beings had not renounced their normal stage of development on Old Sun and had not undergone their evolution on Earth, we should never have known the birth of language on Earth. In certain respects man should feel deep affection for his native language because it was from motives of love that higher Beings remained behind with him and renounced certain attributes in order that man should be able to evolve in accordance with the decrees of higher wisdom. Just as we must regard "hurrying forward" as a kind of sacrifice, so we must also look upon "remaining behind" at earlier stages of evolution as a kind of sacrifice and we must clearly realize that man could not have acquired certain attributes if such sacrifices had not been made.

Thus we see how two kinds of Beings of different rank work alternately in the etheric body of man and in that of the Folk Spirit in question, namely, the Archangels who have followed a normal development and those Spirits of Form who have remained behind at the Archangel stage and have sacrificed their own evolution in order to implant in man during his life on Earth his native language. They had to be endowed with the power to transform the larynx and the organs of speech in such a way that these organs could manifest physically as speech. National sentiments, national temperament, together with the national language must be seen as the result of the cooperation of these Beings. Language, speech and national characteristics, these can be compassed solely by the Folk Spirits in conjunction with the Spirits of Form, because with their greater energy and superior powers the latter had remained behind at the Archangel stage. Cooperation of this nature takes place therefore in the realms where the Folk Spirits are active. Similar cooperative activity is also to be found in yet another domain.

I pointed out yesterday that other forces also are active—the First Beginnings, the Archai or Spirits of Personality, who during the Earth-existence represent what is called the *Zeitgeist*, the Spirit of the Age. These work in such a way that from their own ego, from their psychic organization, they work into the physical body and thus activate the forces of the physical body. If, at a certain moment, something arises as a result of the activity of the *Zeitgeist*, something manifests itself in the Spirit of an Age which furthers the progress of mankind, we must assume that this corresponds to the utilization of physical forces in our Earth life. A moment's reflection will show that definite prior conditions of a physical order are necessary in order to provide for certain contingencies in the Spirit of the Age. Kepler, Copernicus and Pericles could not possibly have lived in any other age or under other circumstances. Personalities are the product of the specific conditions of their time, conditions which at a definite moment of time are created and determined by the higher Beings working on the physical plane. Now these physical conditions must not be regarded as isolated phenomena, but as particular configurations in the physical constitution of our Earth. Sometimes these configurations stand out in bold relief; at other times, when the Spirit of the Age directs his influence in a certain direction, physical objects will inevitably take on a quite definite pattern. You will recall that on one occasion, when for the first time specially polished lenses were used, some children playing in the glass polisher's workshop assembled them in such a way as to create the optical effect of a telescope, so that the inventor of the telescope, having discovered from observation the underlying principle, only needed to apply it to achieve practical results. This is an historic fact. Imagine the number of physical processes involved before this result could be achieved. The lenses had first of all to be invented, polished and then assembled in the appropriate manner. Chance would account for this, you might say, but only on condition that you refuse to acknowledge the law that operates in such circumstances. This concatenation of outward circumstances is the work of the Archai, the Primal Forces. Their work is the consequence of focussing their activity at a particular place, an activity which otherwise, as Spirit of the Age, is expressed in a variety of ways. Think of how many inventions would remain for ever unknown if this work of the Archai had not taken place in their etheric bodies. It is really the work of the Archai which acts in this way and is directed to this end.

Now if the activity of the Archai takes this form and is responsible for directing the Spirit of the Age, the question arises: how do these Spirits of the Age intuitively sense the progress of mankind? They create a situation in which man appears to be stimulated fortuitously by external circumstances. It must not be accounted as pure fiction if this sometimes occurs. I need only remind you of the swinging lamp in the cathedral at Pisa where, by observing the regular oscillations of the lamp, Galileo discovered the law of the pendulum and how, later on, Kepler and Newton were stimulated to make their discoveries. I could quote innumerable cases of the coincidence of external events and human thought which would explain how the prevailing ideas of an age are intuitively sensed by the Archai, ideas which influence man's development, determine his progress and subject it to law. In this domain also, those Beings who have normally become Spirits of Personality during our Earth-existence, work in conjunction with other Beings, who, because they remained behind on the Old Moon, are at present not Spirits of Form or Powers as they ought to be on Earth, but are now for the first time working as Spirits of Personality.

Thus those Beings who remained behind in their evolution not at the Old Sun stage, but only at the Old Moon stage, are now Spirits of Personality. They do not possess the attributes which they should normally have, i.e. they do not "intuit" in the manner of the backward Spirits of Form. They do not stimulate man from without; they work more subtly, they leave it to man himself to observe the changes in his physical being; they stimulate inwardly, fashion the inner configuration of the brain and encourage a certain trend of thought. Hence the thought-life of man at different epochs is motivated from within, so that each epoch has its own definite mode of thought. This depends upon the delicate configurations of the thought-life, upon its inner patterns. Here the backward Spirits of Form who preserve the characteristics of the Spirits of Personality work within man and create a certain way of thinking, a quite specific pattern of ideas. Thus, from epoch to epoch, man is not only guided according to the will of the intuiting Spirits of Personality who induce him of his own volition to follow a certain course of action, but he is impelled as if by inner forces, so that thought starts from within and manifests itself externally in a physical form, just as language, on the other hand, is a manifestation of the backward Spirits of Form. Thus the way of thinking is an expression of those Spirits of Form who in our age are known as Spirits of Personality. These are not, therefore, Spirits of Personality who work in a subtle and intimate way and leave man to his own devices; they take possession of him and drive him irresistibly on. Hence you can always find in those men who are stimulated by the Spirit of the Age, these two types. Those persons who are stimulated by the true Spirits of the Age at their normal stage of development are the true representatives of their time. We can look upon them as men who were destined to appear; we feel certain that their activities were predestined. There are also others, however, in whom are active those Spirits of Personality who are, in reality, Spirits of Form. Those are the Spirits whom we called the 'Thought Spirits', who during the Old Moon cycle advanced to their present rank. Man is the stage upon which the activities of these Beings are coordinated. This is demonstrated by the mutual interaction between language and thought, by the reciprocal relationship not only between the Spirits at the same stage of development, but also by the reciprocal relationship between the normal Archangels who determine national sentiment and temperament and those just described— i.e. not only between the Spirits of Form who are at the Archangel stage, but also between those Spirits of Personality who, in reality, are 'backward' Spirits of Form.

These two kinds of Beings are reflected in the make-up and being of man. It is extremely interesting to observe this relationship when, with occult knowledge and insight, we study the different peoples. We are then able to follow the way in which the normal Folk Spirits work and take their directions from the Spirits of the Age; how these Folk Spirits work in the inner being of man in conjunction with the Spirits of language and also with the Spirits of thought who work into the thoughts of man. Within man there are not only normal and abnormal Archangels, but also the Archangels in contrast to the abnormal Spirits of Personality who from within determine the pattern of thought of a particular epoch. I have already mentioned that I proposed to touch upon conditions which you must accept with your spiritual understanding and which must be clothed in ordinary language because no language has as yet been invented which would make all this clear and credible. I am therefore obliged to use a terminology which is somewhat figurative. None the less my description of the situation accords with an important fact in the evolution of mankind. It is most interesting and instructive to follow the evolution of humanity in recent times and to discover that a mutual agreement was once arrived at between one of the guiding Folk Spirits who is a normal Archangel, and an abnormal Spirit of Personality who works in the inner being of man as Spirit of the Thought-forces. The far-reaching consequences of this agreement is reflected in a particular epoch of history. In order to make this agreement fully effective a harmonious relationship was established with the corresponding normal Archangel who was the guiding Spirit of language at that time. Thus there was a moment in the evolution of mankind when the normal and abnormal Archangels worked together and when, furthermore, the mode of thinking which was brought about from within by an abnormal Spirit of Personality, was super-added. The harmonious relationship between these spiritual Beings is reflected in the ancient Indians of the first post-Atlantean epoch. It was owing to the concatenation of circumstances at the time of the ancient Indian culture that these Beings were able to work in closest harmony. This is the source of the historical rôle of the Indian people. The prolonged effects of this concerted action could still be felt in those later epochs when records of ancient Indian tradition were still extant. That is the reason why the sacred Sanscrit language exercised such a powerful influence and had such telling effects upon culture, both in the past and in later epochs. This power was the work of the Archangels who were responsible for language. The strength of the Sanscrit language depends upon that harmonious relationship of Beings of which I have just spoken. It accounts for the uniqueness of Indian philosophy which, as creative thought expressive of the inner life, is unsurpassed by any other people, and it also explains the inner perfection of thought so characteristic of the Indian culture. In all other continents different conditions prevailed. The picture I have just presented refers only to the Indian culture of that epoch. Hence it is so infinitely fascinating to follow up these trains of thought which assume their characteristic pattern because they have resulted, not from the predominance of the normal Archangel over the abnormal Archangel, but from the harmonious interaction of these Beings, because every thought was literally assimilated by the temperament of the people and elaborated with loving care at the time when the Indian people represented the first flowering of the post-Atlantean culture. And the language preserved its powerful influence because conflict had not arisen there which otherwise might have arisen, because the normal and abnormal Archangels

4—MOFS * *

acted in concert. Thus language, the spontaneous overflow of a pure, uncorrupted temperament, is itself an expression of that temperament. That is the sercret of the first post-Atlantean civilization.

And we must also bear in mind that in all other peoples these Beings or forces cooperate in their diverse ways—the normal Folk Spirit or Archangel, the abnormal Archangel and the abnormal Time Spirit who works through the brain (working not as a normal Time Spirit, but from within the body); and finally the true Time Spirit who transmits intuitively the thought-life to the people. We shall really understand a people when we feel intuitively the activity of these Beings or forces and estimate the contribution each makes to the constitution of a people. It is difficult, therefore, for those who do not take into consideration the occult forces in the evolution of mankind, to provide a satisfactory definition of the word 'folk'. If you look up the word 'folk' or 'people' in a book on ethnology you will find the strangest assortment of definitions. The authors must of necessity give different interpretations because one will respond more to what stems from the normal Archangels, another to what stems from the abnormal Archangels and a third to what stems from the several personalities of the people. Each has a different response which will modify his definition. But we have learned through Spiritual Science that these definitions need not of necessity be false; they are simply subject to maya or illusion. A writer's statements will betray how far he is the victim of Maya or how far he has left out of account the various forces at work. If, from the anthroposophical standpoint, we compare a people such as the Swiss who occupy the same territory and are tri-lingual with peoples who are unilingual we shall inevitably have widely different conceptions of what constitutes a people.

We shall discuss later why it is that in some peoples the Spirit of Personality is the more active agent, that is, why their mode of life is determined by the cooperation of the several personalities. We shall also meet with peoples on Earth whose life is largely determined by the abnormal Spirit of Personality. These Spirits of Personality do not contribute to the further development of the peoples. A study of the character of the North American people shows a people who, for the time being, are under an abnormal Spirit of Personality. We shall therefore only understand world-history, in so far as it consists of the history of peoples, if we observe the normal and abnormal Archangels, the normal and abnormal Spirits of Personality in their mutual relationships and cooperative activity and at the same time follow up their influence upon the successive peoples in the course of the world's history.

LECTURE THREE

The inner Life of the Folk Spirits. Formation of the Races.

In the course of these lectures we shall undertake investigations that will readily strike a responsive chord in all of you because they will stimulate your immediate and lively interest. But since the picture would otherwise be incomplete we must first embark upon such enquiries as are necessary in order to ensure a full and complete understanding and which you will find rather more difficult to grasp than the central theme of our lectures. Today, for instance, we shall be obliged to turn our attention to the inner life of the normal Folk Spirits, those Archangelic Beings of whom we have spoken in the two preceding lectures.

We have already described them in their external aspect as Beings two stages beyond man, Beings who, at the present time, are engaged in transmuting their etheric bodies into Buddhi or Life Spirit. Now man is also involved in this activity. In so far as he is involved in the progressive evolution of these Archangelic Beings, this Folk Spirit is reflected in the human individuality itself as the folk-characteristic of the individual human being.

We must now look a little more closely into the inner life of the Folk Soul. If we wish to throw light upon the inner being of man today, we must picture it as composed of three members:

the Sentient Soul which is the lowest member,
the Intellectual Soul or Mind-Soul, the central member, and
the Spiritual Soul or Consciousness-Soul, the highest member,
   in which the human ego first becomes conscious.

Self-consciousness is first developed in the Spiritual Soul. Nevertheless the 'I' of man is active in all three members of his inner life, in the Sentient Soul, in the Intellectual or Mind-Soul and in the Spiritual Soul (Consciousness-Soul).

In the Sentient Soul man is hardly aware of his ego and in consequence is the victim of his passions and desires. The 'I' stirs feebly in the Sentient Soul, struggles to free itself, emerges for the first time in the Intellectual Soul and only becomes fully conscious in the Spiritual Soul. If we wish to examine these three members of the inner being of man independently of each other, we must regard them as three modifications, as three members of the astral body. These modifications prepare the transformation of the astral body itself, of the etheric body and of the physical body. These transformations, however, are not to be confused with the real inner being of man. The psychic life, the inner being of man, consists of three modifications of the astral body. The three modifications can manifest themselves only through the agency of the lower bodies—the Sentient Soul through the astral body, the Intellectual Soul through the etheric body and the Spiritual Soul through the physical body. We can thus distinguish the inner being of man from his outer sheath or envelope. Man's inner being therefore consists of three modifications of the astral body.

Just as man's inner life which is the field of ego-activity is manifested in these three modifications of the astral body, so the true inner life of the Folk Spirits, or that which corresponds to the inner life of man, is manifested in three members, three modifications of the etheric body. In man we distinguish Sentient Soul, Intellectual Soul, Spiritual Soul; in the Archangelic Beings, the normal Folk Spirits, we distinguish three modifications of the etheric body and since these three modifications are situated not in the astral, but in the etheric body, they differ fundamentally from the three modifications in the soul-life of man. Therefore, you must think of the form of consciousness, of the entire soul-life of these Folk Spirits, as different from that of man. Let us now turn aside from an external description to look more closely into the inner life of these Folk Spirits. That will not be very easy, but we must be prepared to make the endeavour. We must take our starting-point from some familiar conception, a conception that bears a close relation to the inner life of the Folk Spirits. In the normal life of man such conceptions are few and far between; man's consciousness has very little in common with that

of the Folk Spirits. It may help you towards an understanding of
the consciousness of the Folk Spirits if you will bear with me in the
following observation.

Now you have all learnt at school that the sum of the three
angles of a triangle is equal to two right angles. You know that
this axiom could not in any way be demonstrated from external
experience. Picture, for example, the wooden or metallic triangles in your box of geometrical instruments. If you measure
the three angles of a triangle with the aid of a protractor you
will never discover from external experience alone that the sum of
these three angles is equal to 180°. But, irrespective of whether
you construct a triangle or merely imagine it, you will know at
once from inner experience that the sum of the three angles is 180°.
This must be an inner experience, it must spring from the inner
power of your own soul. In order to realize this one need only
reconstruct mentally the following. (The diagram is intended
only as a symbolic representation of the thought.)

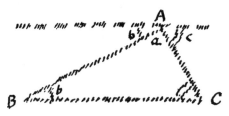

This figure shows conclusively that the sum of the three
angles is equal to two right angles. You need only visualize this
figure and it will confirm this axiom for all triangles. You
can hold this figure in your mind's eye without the need to
draw it. You thus perform an operation in pure thought by the
power of your own inner activity; there is no need to go outside
yourself. You can imagine for a moment that the world of
sensation and the world of sense-impressions no longer exist.
Imagine the external world as non-existent and space a creation of
thought; then, in this space, the sum-total of the angles of every
triangle would amount to 180°. In order to arrive at geometrical
and mathematical knowledge sense-data are superfluous; inner
experience, what takes place in consciousness itself, suffice.

I selected this example because it is the simplest and most practical, and confirms what people have learnt at school. I could also give you the example of Hegelian logic, which would also provide you with a number of inner concepts. But here you would find much with which you are unfamiliar, since Hegelian logic is only known to the few. From this it is evident that man can arrive at knowledge purely from within, without the stimulus of external motivation.

If you can imagine that which can only be arrived at externally through the logic of mathematics you will have some idea of how the consciousness of the Archangels works. They do not perceive the external world of colours and tones, such as the ordinary man experiences. These sensations are unknown to a Being of this kind; it is impossible for him to receive tactile impressions of objects. Such experiences are foreign to him. But his experiences can be expressed in these words: 'Something is now streaming into me from the world of inspiration and this inspiration permeates my consciousness and takes full possession of it'.

Now the Archangels are not Beings who are limited to mathematical concepts only; rather is it the consequence of man's limitations that he can only conceive of the activity of the Archangels in terms of abstractions, such as the truths of mathematics. These truths are the normal experiences both of man and the Folk Spirits. From this you may infer that the Archangels are not interested in the phenomenal world perceived through the senses. The external world as experienced by man, and his sense-derived knowledge of that world, is a world unknown to the Archangels. If you exclude, therefore, from your picture of the world all sensations and perceptions of the physical world, then you exclude precisely that which does not concern the Archangels. The question then is: what facet of consciousness is still common to man and the Archangels, to the Folk Spirits? All experiences of the Sentient Soul, the normal joys or sorrows of life, all colours and sounds, in fact all sensory perceptions of the external world —none of this concerns these Beings. Eliminate therefore the entire contents of the Sentient Soul of man and remember that the world-picture which is the product of the Sentient Soul is of no importance to the Archangels; they cannot participate in it.

Even one part of the Intellectual Soul that is stimulated by external sensations has no significance for the Archangels. That which is triggered off by external motivation, man's intellectual preoccupations and emotional experiences, these too do not concern the Archangels. But in the Intellectual Soul of man there are, however, certain things which he experiences in common with the Archangels. We are fully aware of this when we see, for example, how our moral ideals are born within us. There would be no moral ideals if our sentient responses, our joys and sorrows and our thought-life were dependent upon our sense-perceptions of the external world. In that event no doubt we might delight in the flowers of the field or in a beautiful land-scape, but our hearts could never be fired with enthusiasm for an ideal that may illumine us from beyond the external world, an ideal that we can inscribe in our hearts and to which we are passionately devoted. But we must not only glow with enthusiasm and respond with sensibility in the Sentient Soul; we must also learn to reflect. The person who only feels and does not think may well be an enthusiast, but he is never a practical man. We must not receive ideals into our Sentient Soul from outside; we must allow them to stream into us from out of the spiritual world and we must work upon them in the intellectual or Mind-Soul. Artistic and architectural ideals and so on are present in the Intellectual Soul and in the Spiritual Soul. They are related to that which man cannot perceive externally, but which pervades and illumines his inner being so that it becomes a part of his life.

As we follow the life of peoples from epoch to epoch we note how new ideas have continually arisen and how new sources of hidden knowledge have been revealed from time to time. From what source could the Greeks have taken their conceptions of Zeus and Athene if they had relied solely upon external percept-ion? Everything that is included in the traditional wisdom, in the mythologies, religions and sciences of peoples was born of inner spiritual experience. Thus one half of our inner life, that of our Intellectual Soul and of our Spiritual Soul is nourished from within. Indeed to the extent to which man is inwardly permeated with what I have just described, to that extent the Archangels can penetrate into the inner being of man and this defines the extent of their actual participation. You must therefore exclude from the inner life that which the Sentient Soul receives from outside and which the Intellectual Soul elaborates. Then we come to the 'Ego' which to us is the highest member of our being. What we introduce into our moral consciousness are ideals, moral and aesthetic ideals. Whilst man's perception of the inner world is screened from him, he is able through the medium of the senses to perceive the external world of colours, sounds, cold and warmth. At the same time he is aware that behind these colours, sounds, warmth and cold there exists a fundamental reality, namely, the Beings of the animal, plant and mineral kingdoms. And so man can think of the world in the way I have indicated as having continuity in higher realms. The vision of these higher realms is denied the ordinary person and it is this loss of vision that accounts for the growth of materialism. If man could have a clear view over the realm extending beyond the Intellectual Soul and Spiritual Soul, then it would be as foolish to doubt the existence of the spiritual world as it would be foolish today to doubt the existence of the animal, plant and mineral kingdoms.

You will recall how man's 'I', his highest member, embraces the Sentient, Intellectual and spiritual Souls. Now the soul-life of the Archangel first begins with the existence of its soul-life in the Intellectual or Mind-Soul; it then rises into the 'I' which embraces a world of higher realms, a realm of spiritual realities in which it dwells, as man dwells in the kingdom of the animals, plants and minerals. We must realize therefore that the soul-life of this Archangelic Being may possess what we call human 'I'; nevertheless the ego of the Archangel is not of the same nature, it is not identical with the human 'I'. The 'I' of the Archangel is, in fact, two stages higher, so that the Archangel and his 'I' are rooted in a higher world. Just as man sees colours and hears sounds by means of his sense-perception, so the Archangel looks down upon the world that embraces the 'I' as objective truth; but around this 'I' is still gathered some of that part of the astral nature which we human beings call the Intellectual or Mind-Soul. Think of these Beings as gazing into a world which does not extend to minerals, plants and animals. Instead of this, imagine their spiritual gaze to be directed towards their world-picture and that they perceive therein centres or focal points. These centres are the human egos around which again is gathered something that appears as a kind of aura. This picture illustrates how the Archangelic Being looks down upon those personalities of the folk belonging to him and who constitute his particular people. His world consists of an astral field of perception in which there are certain centres; these centres, these focal points, are the individual human personalities, the individual human egos. Just as to us colours, sounds, warmth and cold lie within our field of perception and constitute a world of reality, so to the Archangelic Beings, to the Folk Spirits, we ourselves with a part of our inner life are their field of perception; and just as we set out to conquer nature and transform it to serve our purposes, so we, in our turn, in so far as we belong to a particular Folk Spirit, are the raw material to be moulded by the Archangels or Folk Spirits.

Thus we gain insight, strange as it may appear, into a higher epistemology of the Archangels. This is entirely different from the epistemology of man; the Archangels start from a datum of a different order. For man the datum is everything appertaining to spatial extension and which we know through sensory apprehension as colour, sound, warmth, cold, hardness and softness. The datum for Archangels is what appears in the field of human consciousness; to them that is an aggregate of centres or focal points round which the inner experiences of man are grouped, in so far as these experiences take place in the Intellectual or Mind-Soul. Their activity is, by comparison, of a higher order.

What are the specific characteristics of the world of the Archangels or Folk Spirits? The world of man is characterized by the fact that he feels an object to be warm or cold when he takes hold of it. The Archangel experiences something similar when he meets with human individualities. He meets with some who respond more actively to the quickening powers of the soul, men with a richer inner life; these make a deeper impression on him. Others he finds casual, lethargic, psychically empty. He feels them as warm or cold respectively, just as the human soul responds to impressions of warmth and cold. Such are the characteristics of the world of the Archangel who, according to circumstances, can make use of the individual men and work on their behalf by weaving out of his own being that which has to guide the whole people. But there is another way in which the life of this Archangel is related to the life of the particular people he is leading. Just as the graph of man's life shows an ascending an descending curve, the springtime of youth and the winter of old age, so the Archangel experiences his youth and old age in the rise and fall of a people's culture.

We must now look again into the inner life of such an Archangel. From what I have said you will have observed no doubt that what man receives from without, the Archangel receives from within; hence when the Archangel experiences the individual members of a people as centres within him, he feels that this experience does, in effect, originate in his consciousness, but nevertheless is alien to him. It resembles the sudden ideas that flash into our consciousness—its influence upon him is in inverse proportion to the influence of youth and age upon man. In youth man feels his limbs to be young and supple, to be growing and developing. In old age they become flaccid and atrophy That is something which man feels to be an expression of his organic life. Now the Archangel, it is true, feels everything to be an expression of his inner life, but the rise and fall of a nation nevertheless seems something foreign to him. It is something which he feels to be independent of him and for which he is not directly responsible, but which gives him the occasion to incarnate in a particular people at a definite time. When the opportunity for incarnation occurs, when a people can be found in the full vigour of youth, in the creative period of its life, then the Archangel incarnates in that people just as man incarnates after passing through the period between death and rebirth. Equally the Archangel senses his impending death, feels the need to withdraw from the people in question when he perceives the individual centres beginning to be less productive, less active and to lose their inner vitality. Then comes the time when he withdraws from the particular national community, enters into his Devachan, the life between death and rebirth, in order on a later occasion to seek out another community. Thus the springtime of a people, its youthful vigour and vitality testifies to the youth of the Folk

Spirit, which he experiences as a living, vitalizing force within him. He experiences the decline of the life of a people as the withering of the centres in his inner field of perception. This should give to some extent an insight into the inner being of a particular Folk Soul.

In the light of this information we may say that in certain respects a Folk Soul is rather far removed from the individual human being, for man's Sentient Soul and the lower part of his Intellectual Soul are beyond the immediate perception of the Folk Spirit or Archangel. For man, however, it is something very real, something that he feels to be intimately associated with the very core of his own life. In a certain respect the Archangel Being, the guiding Spirit of a nation, is something which hovers above the individual members. Man's personal experiences which derive from his sense-perceptions are wholly foreign to the Archangel who is guiding the people. But there are intermediaries, and it is important that we should realize that such intermediaries exist. They are the Beings we call Angels and they mediate between Archangels and man. You must understand quite literally, that Folk Spirits are Archangels, Spirits who have completed the transformation of their astral bodies into Spirit Self or Manas and are now in process of transmuting their etheric body into Life Spirit. Intermediate between those Beings and man are the Angels. These are Beings who are engaged in transmuting their astral body into Spirit Self or Manas, but have not yet completed their task. At the present time man stands at the initial stage of this task; the Angels are nearing the end of this task but are by no means finished with it. Therefore these Beings are more closely related to the life and activities of man; with their whole soul-nature they feel more drawn to the astral body. Hence they have the fullest understanding for the joys and sorrows of man. But because they possess a higher Ego than the human ego, because they are able to reach up into the higher worlds, their consciousness extends into those spheres where the consciousness of the Archangels is active. They are therefore the true intermediaries between the Archangels and the individual human being. They transmit the behests of the Folk Spirits to the individual souls and thereby help to determine what the individual can do, not only for his own evolution, but for his whole people.

In the life of man these two streams flow side by side. The one stream carries him forward from incarnation to incarnation—it is concerned with his personal destiny, which he has to fulfil in order to discharge that duty which is to him the most solemn and sacred because it is peculiarly his own. He cannot afford to stand still because his latent capacities would otherwise lie fallow if he failed to cultivate them. Such is his individual destiny by virtue of which he progresses from incarnation to incarnation.

But his contribution to his own people, all that touches upon the affairs of his immediate community, stems from the inspiration of the Angel who transmits the behests of the Archangel to the individual.

We can easily picture therefore a people inhabiting a certain territory; over this people extends the etheric aura of the people into which the forces of the Folk Spirit work, modifying the etheric body of man in accordance with the three types of force. In this Folk-aura the Archangel is at work. We must think of him as a higher Being, two stages higher than man in evolution, hovering over the whole people, issuing directives concerning what this people as a whole has to fulfil. The Archangel knows what steps must be undertaken during the creative period of a people when its youthful vigour and vitality are strongest. He knows what aims must be pursued by a people during the period of transition from youth to age in order that his directives may function in the right way.

This grandiose plan is the work of the Archangels. Here on the physical plane the individual human being must ensure that these great aims are realized. Between the individual and the Archangels are the Angels who mediate between them. The Angels impel him towards the locality ordained for him, so that the feelings of the people should concur in the great ordinances of the Archangels. We shall see this in the proper perspective if we take what I have been describing not simply as an allegory, but as a close approximation to reality.

Now the whole pattern of events woven by the Archangels is

subject to the influence of the abnormal Archangels, the Spirits of
language, as I described yesterday. We have also described how
the abnormal Spirits of Personality, the Archai, exercise their
influence. We can now turn our attention to the domain in which
the Archangels issue their directives, in which they apportion the
various tasks which are then transmitted by the Angels to the
separate individuals. But the Archangels are also able to work into
the sphere of the abnormal Spirits of Personality, and in the
mutual cooperation of the Archangels with the abnormal Spirits
of Personality—since the latter are pursuing totally different
aims—it is possible that the plans of the Archangels are in
certain respects frustrated. When this occurs, when these abnormal Spirits of Personality thwart the designs of the Archangels,
groups with specially appointed tasks arise within the nation
itself. Under these circumstances the activity of the Spirits of
Personality is visible externally. This may last for centuries. In
Germany, for example, where there is an urgent need today for
anthroposophical work, you have seen for centuries this interplay
of the Archangel of the Germans and the sometimes opposing
separate Spirits of Personality. The fragmentation of the one
German nation into the many smaller ethnic groups illustrates
the interplay of the abnormal Spirits of Personality with the
Archangel.

Nations like this are little centralized, they look more to the
development of individuality. In some ways this is good, for a
variety of shades within the national character can thereby find
expression.

One may also take the other case where not the abnormal Spirit
of Personality, but the normal Spirit of Personality expressing
himself in the Spirit of the Age, assumes for a certain time greater
importance than would normally follow from the ordinary
course of events.

In studying a people we regard the Archangel as its guiding
principle. Then follows the influence of the Spirit of the Age who
gives his directives to the Archangel of the different nations and
these in turn give them to the Angels who transmit them to the
separate individuals. Because, as a rule, we see only what is
obvious, so in this concerted action the activity of the Archangels

is seen to be the most important element. Circumstances, however, may arise when the Spirit of the Age has to issue more important, more momentous directives, when he is compelled, so to speak, to take over some of the authority of the Archangel, because he must detach a portion of the people in order that the task of the Age, the mission of the Spirit of the Age may be fulfilled. In such a case national groups split off from the rest; the Spirit of the Age visibly gains the upper hand over the influence of the Archangel. A case in point occurred when the Dutch people severed its connection with the kindred German people. Holland and Germany shared originally an Archangel in common; the separation occurred because the Spirit of the Age detached a portion of the people at a given moment and then transferred to this portion what have become the vital interests of the modern Spirit of the Age. Dutch history is simply a reflection of this inner process—in reality all history is only an external expression, a Maya, of an inner process. In the present case we see the separation of the Dutch people from the common Teutonic stock taking place externally. But the inner reality is that the Spirit of the Age required an instrument with which to fulfil his mission overseas. The entire mission of the Dutch people was in the hands of the Spirit of the Age. The purpose of the separation was to enable the Spirit of the Age to enlist this portion of the people in his service in order to execute important tasks at a specific moment in history. What is described by the historians is only Maya; it conceals rather than reveals the true facts.

You can meet with other examples which afford a striking illustration of this situation, namely, the severance of Portugal from Spain, where a portion of the people had to separate from the main body of the people. You may look in vain for other explanations; you will find that in this case it is simply a question of a victory of the Spirit of the Age over the Archangel. If you analyse the events individually you will find that the opportunity was taken—and such opportunities were few and far between— to form a special people. The Spanish people formed with the Portuguese a homogeneous group. The external reason for this severance was perhaps that the rivers were only navigable up to the Portuguese frontiers. There is no other geographical explanation. The inner reason, on the other hand, was that the specific tasks which had to be fulfilled by the Portuguese were different from those of the united Spanish people. Here we see the Spirits of the Age developing a more intense activity than they normally display. The harmony which had prevailed hitherto is replaced by a new relationship. Instead of giving his directives to the Archangel, the Spirit of the Age intervenes directly in the history of the people, and other Spirits seize this opportunity to incarnate. When such a people is detached from its racial group, then, in that initial enthusiasm which overtakes the individual members of that people, the Spirit of the Age discharges for a time the functions of the Archangel so completely that scarcely any evidence of the severance survives save an atmosphere of bustling excitement and ferment in this people. This vigour and vitality, this spirit of objectivity, stem from the mission of the Spirit of the Age. Then a normal and abnormal Archangel have the opportunity to incarnate in that section of the people which has broken away. Thus we see the growth of the Dutch and Portuguese peoples who are now under the guidance of their own normal and abnormal Archangels. And the influence of these spiritual Beings is seen in the difference in temperament which is reflected in the individual personalities of these two peoples. The work of these spiritual Beings is quite remarkable, and we now recognize that the external events of history are simply an expression of their activity.

Gradually the saying that the external world is Maya or illusion is seen to have increasing importance. The external events of history are simply the outer reflection of the supersensible Beings, just as man is the outer reflection of the inner man. For this reason I had to insist, and I must emphasize this again and again, that the saying 'the world is Maya' is so vitally important. It is not sufficient to emphasize this in an abstract way; we must be in a position to apply it to every aspect of life.

Now, as we know, other Spirits and Hierarchies are active in the world. We have already spoken of the normal and abnormal Archangels. The abnormal Archangels have shown themselves to be, in reality, Spirits of Form or Powers who have only renounced in part the attributes of their evolution. The question that now arises is: what is the position of the normal Spirits of Form? The normal Spirits of Form are four stages beyond man—we shall have more to say about them in our next lecture. In the hierarchial order mentioned yesterday the Spirits of Form do not occupy the highest rank. Above them are the Spirits of Movement, Dynamis or Mights; beyond these again are the Spirits of Wisdom, Kyriotetes. I have referred to these different spiritual Beings in my books, *Cosmic Memory* and *Occult Science—an Outline*.

Now you must understand that the law of renunciation, of deferred development, applies also to the higher Beings, that the Spirits of Movement who are five stages beyond man may also remain behind with certain attributes, that certain Spirits of Movement are today bound up with human evolution as if they were now only Spirits of Form or Powers. In respect of certain attributes they are really Spirits of Movement, whereas in respect of other attributes which they have sacrificed, they are Spirits of Form. Thus there are normal Spirits of Form four stages beyond man and other Beings working in the same sphere as the Spirits of Form, but who are really Spirits of Movement. Just as there is a sphere in which the normal and abnormal Archangels cooperate so we have here a sphere in which the normal and abnormal Spirits of Form, the abnormal Spirits of Movement, cooperate. Through this interplay are formed the races of mankind. Race must not be confused with nation.

If we approach the matter in this light we shall avoid confusion and our ideas will be more elastic. A nation is not a race. The concept of nation has nothing to do with that of race. A race may be divided into many different nations; races are different from folk communities. We rightly speak of a German, Dutch or Norwegian nation; at the same time we speak of a Germanic race. Now what lies behind the concept of race? Those Beings whom we describe as normal Spirits of Form work in conjunction with those Beings whom we have come to know as the abnormal Spirits of Form, but who are Spirits of Movement in reality, entrusted with the mission of Spirits of Form. This is the reason why mankind is divided into races. That which gives man his human stature, which makes every man, irrespective of his race, a member of the human species—this is the work of the normal Spirits of Form. That which divides the whole of mankind into races is the work of the abnormal Spirits of Form who made an act of renunciation so that instead of a single human family a wide diversity of types could exist on Earth.

Thus we gain an insight into the spiritual background from which the individual peoples emerge and are thus able to follow their evolution over the whole Earth. We find that, by virtue of the normal Spirits of Form, one common Humanity should exist on Earth; that the backward Spirits of Movement enter into the sphere belonging to the Spirits of Form and as abnormal Spirits of Form are responsible for differentiating mankind the whole world over into races. When we look into the purposes of these Spirits, when we inquire closely into the aims and objects of these normal and abnormal Spirits of Form, then we shall understand the designs they entertain for the races of mankind and how through these races a foundation is laid for that which shall emerge from them. If we take the example of a particular people and study it, then, in the light of what we have said, we shall have understood and comprehended this people.

LECTURE FOUR

The Evolution of Races and Civilization.

If we wish to understand the relationship of the races of mankind to one another and the origins of the individual folk communities, we must realize that man as we know him today is a highly
complex being and that his present form and inner being could
only have arisen through the cooperation of countless numbers
of cosmic Beings. From the study of the 'Akashic Record' and
other observations on the evolution of man we know that in
prehistoric times our Earth, before reaching its present condition,
had to pass through three conditions, in the course of which
the three so-called members or vehicles of man, the physical
body, the etheric body and the astral body were prefigured,
gradually realized and developed until they reached their present
state. It is only during his present Earth incarnation that man has
been able to develop a fourth member, an ego. These four
members testify to the activity of the spiritual Beings during the
three or four incarnations of our Earth—Old Saturn, Old Sun,
Old Moon and the Earth period itself up to the present moment.
If you will call to mind all the Beings who worked together during
those incarnations, the Spirits of Will or Thrones, the Spirits
of Wisdom, of Movement, of Form, of Personality, the Archangels down to the Angels—and above the Thrones, the
Cherubim and Seraphim—it is clear that man's present organization could only have been created through a complex interplay of spiritual forces. We have seen that not only was the
cooperation of many Beings and nature-forces in the Cosmos
a necessity, but that for the creation of man it was also necessary
that at certain epochs, certain Beings should renounce the normal
course of their evolution and remain behind in order to be able
to participate in the organization of man in a way that

would have been impossible in the normal course of their evolution.

And so when we seek to understand man as he is today, we find a richly varied and many patterned fabric. Only when we examine this fabric closely and watch the activity of the several Beings do we begin to understand how man first came into existence through the cooperation of these Beings. The chief Being who is of importance for contemporary man is the one who has gradually made ego-consciousness possible. The opportunity to develop ego-consciousness was first provided by the Spirits of Form, the Beings whom we call Powers or Exusiai. If we follow the activity of these Beings alone and ask ourselves how man would fare if the normal Spirits alone were predominantly active in him, we shall find that they are the donors of the ego-organization. And this implies that their chief interest is to further man's ego-development which can only be realized in the man of today at a certain age.

If you recall the teachings of Spiritual Science on the subject of the education of the child you will know that in the first seven-year period of life, between birth and the change of teeth, man develops principally the physical body. The Spirits of Form have no particular interest in the development of the physical body since this is really a recapitulation of what man underwent on Old Saturn (which has often been repeated) and which from the last physical birth up to the age of seven has for the time being been recapitulated in a particular way for the last time. The second seven-years period of life from the ages of seven to fourteen, the age of puberty, is also a period which holds little interest for the Spirits of Form since it is a recapitulation of what man underwent on Old Sun. In reality the Spirits of Form only wished to embark on their chief activity, the bestowal of an ego, during man's life on Earth. The third seven-year period covers the years between fifteen and twenty-one. During this period man recapitulates the development of the astral body that normally belongs to the Old Moon epoch. And again the normal Spirits of Form show no interest. The three life-periods, then, that precede the actual birth of the ego at the age of twenty approximately, have no immediate appeal. The Spirits of Form only intervene on their own initiative at the age of twenty approximately. On reflection, therefore, you will not be surprised to learn that the Spirits of Form intended, in fact, that man should incarnate only at the normal developmental stage of twenty or thereabouts.

In the eyes of these Spirits of Form all that has been developed in man hitherto is, in reality, a kind of embryonic state, a sort of germinal condition. And if I may speak somewhat figuratively I might say that the Spirits of Form who have developed normally would far prefer it if things proceeded with almost clock-work regularity, if hitherto no-one encroached upon their province. If these Spirits of Form had free rein until man's twentieth year, then in the first seven years of his life man would have the consciousness pertaining to the physical body, namely, the very dim consciousness of the mineral kingdom. In the second seven years, between the ages of seven and fourteen, he would have a sleep-consciousness. From the fourteenth to the twentieth year he would be very active inwardly, but would live in a kind of dreamlike consciousness of the Old Moon evolution. Not until the age of twenty-one approximately would he awaken to ego-consciousness. If he followed the normal course of development therefore he would only awaken to ego-consciousness at that age and perceive the external world in the form that is familiar to us today.

If we only take into account the activity of the Spirits of Form it is clear that man attains his present-day consciousness much too early. Now in modern man this consciousness, as you know, awakens to some extent soon after birth. He would not develop a clear and distinct perception of the external world if other Spirits, in reality Spirits of Movement, had not remained behind and renounced the development of certain capacities which they could otherwise have acquired up to the time of the Earth-evolution, so that they could intervene in man's development in a particular way during this present Earth-evolution. Because their evolution followed a different path they are in a position to bestow upon man prematurely that which he ought to acquire only in his twentieth year approximately. These are spiritual Beings who renounced the possibility of continuing their evolution normally up to the stage of their Earth-evolution, Beings who might have been Spirits of Movement during the Earth-evolution, but who remained at the stage of the Spirits of Form and are now active in the Earth-evolution as Spirits of Form. Thus they are able, during the Earth-evolution, to bestow upon man, who is by no means mature enough to receive it and has much to redeem from an earlier epoch, the ego-consciousness that would normally be his only around the age of twenty. Hence the abnormal Spirits of Form endow man with capacities which otherwise he would have received about his twentieth year only.

The consequences are highly significant. Let us assume for a moment that evolution had followed its normal course. If these abnormal Spirits had not intervened, man would have incarnated on the physical plane in the condition which is natural to him at the age of twenty approximately and would have to go through a totally different embryonic development. Indeed through these abnormal Spirits of Form, man's development from birth to the age of twenty, that is, for about the first third of his life, is subject to the forces of the external world. The first third of our Earth-life therefore is not controlled by spiritual Beings who determine Earth conditions, but by other abnormal spiritual Beings. And because these abnormal Beings participate in evolution, we do not possess therefore the form that we should have if we had incarnated in the condition natural to us at the age of twenty. To compensate for this man must spend the first third of his life (up to the age of twenty) under the powerful influence of these abnormal Beings. In the course of his whole development man is subject to the influence of these abnormal Beings. And the penalty he has to pay for this is that after the middle third of life which is under the influence of normal Spirits of Form only, a progressive decline sets in and the etheric and astral organizations begin to disintegrate. Life therefore is divided into three periods or thirds—an ascending third, a middle third and a descending third. It is only in the middle third that man is a fully integrated person in his Earth-life. In the last third of his life man has to give back what he received during the first, the ascending third; he must repay the debt in kind.

If man had been wholly subject to the influence of the normal
Spirits of Form all that he experiences today up to the twentieth
year would take on a different complexion, a totally different
form. The situation would have been totally different, so that
everything associated with the development of man during the
first of his three life-periods is fundamentally an anticipation of
much that belongs to the later epochs. In consequence, up to
the second life-period man has become a more material being
than he would otherwise have been. He would have experienced
up to this time purely spiritual conditions and would have
incarnated on Earth only at that period of his development
which he undergoes in his twentieth or twenty-first year when he
would find himself Earth-bound. We learn from Spiritual
Science that if his development had proceeded in this way man
would have incarnated only in the condition which he now
attains in his twentieth or twenty-first year. He would not have
been able to go through the preceding conditions on Earth; he
would have been obliged to go through them in the spiritual
spheres surrounding the Earth.

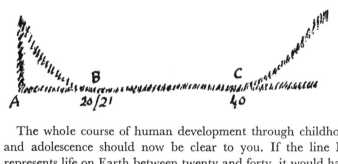

The whole course of human development through childhood
and adolescence should now be clear to you. If the line BC
represents life on Earth between twenty and forty, it would have
been the intention of the Spirits of Form that man should incarnate only at B (the age of twenty to twenty-one). Having come
down to Earth at this age he would have left it again after his
fortieth year (at C) and have spent the last third of his life in a
spiritualized state. Through the abnormal Beings man was
forced to descend upon the Earth at A and begin his life-cycle.
That is the secret of our existence. Thus it is only in the middle
third of life that we are wholly under the influence of these Beings

who actually control us; the periods of our maturity and decline are subject to entirely different Beings who in one way or another have renounced their normal development.

If man had lived through the first and last thirds of his life in the spiritual sphere surrounding the Earth and had incarnated only during the second third, thereby becoming a totally different being, he would not have become Earth-bound to the extent that he is today. If man's development had followed this course, then all those incarnating on Earth would be alike in (physical) form and inner being, they would be standardized. Only a single, uniform humanity would exist. That which determines the racial types with their specific characteristics is unrelated to the middle third of life. Through the circumstances of the earlier years, through the influences of the first third of life, we, with all our forces, are more Earth-bound than the normal Spirits of Form had intended. In consequence man has become more dependent upon the Earth than he would otherwise have been; he has become dependent on the locality where he lives. Because of his premature incarnation—in opposition to the intentions of the Spirits of Form, so to speak—he becomes dependent upon the locality of his birth, he unites with his physical environment in a condition which is not designed for him. It would have been of no consequence whether he had incarnated in the middle third of his life or whether he had been born in the north, south, east or west. But because he has become dependent on his environment, because his youth is lived in the way I have described, he becomes Earth-bound, he becomes closely associated with, and an integral part of the geographical area where he was born. He cannot escape the environmental conditions of that locality— the incidence of the sun's rays, the proximity of the region to the Equator or to a more temperate zone, whether he is born in the lowlands or on a high plateau. The rate of respiration in the plains is different from that in the mountains. Man therefore becomes wholly dependent upon the environmental conditions of his birthplace. He becomes wholly indentified with his native soil through his close association with the locality of his birth. He is moulded by those attributes which he thus receives because these etheric formative forces of the Earth associated with the particular locality where he is born are active in him. All these factors determine his racial character, and the abnormal Spirits of Form, those Spirits or Powers who are responsible for our present consciousness—not between the ages of twenty-one and twenty-three but at some other time—are indirectly the source of the racial differences in mankind everywhere, for these differences depend upon the particular locality where a man is born.

During the first third of life when, in effect, he is under the dominion of the abnormal Spirits of Form, man reaches sexual maturity and develops his capacity for reproduction. His reproductive capacity is acquired during the period when he is not wholly under the direction of the normal Spirits of Form. It is possible therefore that a man is not only dependent on the locality of his birth, but that the characteristics thus acquired may also be inherited by his descendants. Thus racial homogeneity is reflected not only in the influence of the habitat, but also in the racial inheritance. This explains why racial characteristics can be inherited and why, as we shall learn from Spiritual Science, it was only in the past that racial characteristics were determined by the locality where man was born. In the latter part of the Lemurian epoch and in the early Atlantean epoch, for example, man was directly dependent upon his physical environment. In later times race was no longer associated with locality, but was bound up with heredity. In race therefore we see something that was originally associated with a particular geographical region, was later passed on via inheritance, but became increasingly independent of a particular locality.

The period of evolution when one can justifiably speak of the idea of race will be clear to you from what I have just said. One cannot speak of race in the true sense of the term before the Lemurian epoch, for only then did man incarnate on Earth. Before that time he lived in the spiritual environment of the Earth. He then incarnated and racial characteristics were hereditary from the beginning of the Atlantean epoch up to our post-Atlantean epoch. We shall learn later how, in our own time, the national characteristics prepare in their turn the break-down of the racial characteristics and begin to eradicate them.

We must carefully avoid seeing evolution in the form of a

perpetually revolving wheel, for this idea which is widely can-
vassed in many a mystical world-view serves only to confuse the
true picture of evolution. If one pictures evolution as a wheel,
revolving round a fixed centre and divided into so many races,
then we fail to grasp that everything is in a state of evolution and
that the races are evolving too. Races are born and will at some
future time cease to exist. They do not repeat themselves in the
same way as Sinnett mistakenly claims in his *Esoteric Buddhism*.
We must look for the origin of racial characteristics in the old
Lemurian epoch; we must follow their propagation down to our
own day; at the same time we must realize that when our fifth
post-Atlantean epoch is superseded by the sixth and seventh,
race as such will have ceased to exist. But if we picture evolution
as the mechanical, steady, continuous revolution of a wheel, then
we carry the picture of a mill-wheel in our mind and have not
the slightest understanding of evolutionary processes.

The evolution of races begins therefore only in the Lemurian
epoch through the activity of the abnormal Spirits of Form, who
permit the etheric forces from the soil to intervene at the locality
where man has to spend the first years of his life. And this
influence is carried over to some extent into his later life because
man is endowed with a memory, through which he still remem-
bers even in his later life, the time spent under the influence of
the abnormal Spirits before his twenty-first year on Earth. Man
would be a totally different being if he were subject only to the
influence of the normal Spirits of Form. Through the influence
of the abnormal Spirits of Form he is dependent upon the
particular locality in which he lives. I have already described
how man departed from the laws of the normal Spirits of Form,
with the result that the locality of his birth during a particular
incarnation was of importance to him.

These relationships will become clearer to us if we take into
account the following factor. To a certain extent the etheric
forces emanating from the soil permeate the human organism so
that man becomes dependent upon the soil of a particular
geographical area. In this connection I should like to refer to
certain regions of the Earth that are connected with the historical

development of the human being. We shall discuss these relationships in more detail later on. I now propose to describe them in general.

Europe

Asia

Africa

Here is for example a point or a centre of cosmic influence situated in the interior of Africa. At this centre are active all those terrestrial forces emanating from the soil which can influence man especially during his early childhood. Later on their influence diminishes; man is less subject to these forces. Nevertheless their formative influences make a powerful impression upon him. The locality where a man lives exercises its most potent influence in early childhood and thereby determines for their whole life those who are completely dependent on these forces, so that the particular locality impresses the characteristics of their early childhood permanently upon them. This is more or less typical of all those who, in respect of their racial character, are determined by the etheric formative forces of the Earth in the neighbourhood of that particular locality. The black or Negro race is substantially determined by these childhood characteristics.

If we now cross over to Asia, we find a point or centre where the formative forces of the Earth impress permanently on man the particular characteristics of later youth or adolescence and determine his racial character. Such races are the yellow and brown races of our time.

If we continue northward and then turn in a westerly direction towards Europe, a third point or centre is reached which permanently impresses upon man the characteristics of his adult life. In this way man is determined by the etheric forces emanating from the Earth. When we look more closely into these separate points or centres we find that they follow a line which takes an unusual direction. These centres still exist today. The centre in Africa corresponds to those terrestrial forces which imprint on man the characteristics of early childhood; the centre in Asia corresponds to those which give man the characteristics of youth, and the corresponding centre in Europe imprints upon man the characteristics of maturity. This is simply a universal law. Since all men in their different incarnations pass through the various races the claim that the European is superior to the black and yellow races has no real validity. In such cases the truth is sometimes veiled, but you see that with the help of Spiritual Science we do after all light upon remarkable truths.

If we continue this line (see diagram) still further westward we come to America, where the forces of old age, of the final third of life, are active. These forces—I beg you not to misunderstand what I am about to say, it only refers to man in so far as he is dependent upon the forces which determine his physical organism, the terrestrial forces of his environment, forces unrelated to his fundamental being—these forces are associated with the decline of man. This line which in reality describes a curve obeys a cosmic law and does in fact exist; it is a reality and expresses the law according to which our Earth acts upon man. The forces which determine man's racial character follow this cosmic pattern. The American Indians died out, not because of European persecutions, but because they were destined to succumb to those forces which hastened their extinction. The destiny of the races and the changes wrought by the forces which are not under the influence of the normal Spirits of Form are determined by the peculiar characteristics of these different centres of cosmic influence. When determining racial characteristics these Spirits work in this way; but in our age the racial character is gradually being overcome. The first steps in this direction were undertaken for the most part in the earliest period of the Earth's history. If we were to go back to the old Lemurian epoch we would find that the very first indications of racial development could be traced back to the regions of present-day Africa and Asia. Later, a migration westward sets in and as we follow westward the forces which determine race we note their decline amongst the American Indians. The death of races begins with their westward migration. In order to seek the rejuvenating forces, races migrate eastward, from Atlantis across Europe to Asia. Then the westward migration is repeated, but on this occasion we witness, not the movement of races but, as it were, a higher stage of racial development of civilizations. Thus in a certain way we see that the evolution of civilizations is characterized by a continuation of the racial development on a higher plane. For instance, the old Indian civilization, the first post-Atlantean civilization, to which we have already given due recognition in this lecture, corresponds to early childhood, the period when man's response to physical nature is still dormant, when he is receptive to the manifestations of a spiritual world. The first Indian civilization is in fact a revelation from spiritual worlds and could only manifest in man because he came under the influence of the terrestrial forces of India to which he had already been subject from earliest times. In the primeval past men owed their racial characteristics to the etheric formative forces of the soil; now, they owed that disposition of soul peculiar to the ancient Indians to their continuous presence in the same geographical region. Through the migration from West to East they received those fresh, youthful forces which made possible the emergence of that peculiar spiritual configuration so typical of the original Indian civilization. Thus a very ancient Indian civilization which has not yet been studied and of which the Indian civilization now known to science is only an offshoot, can be explained by the fact that the Atlantean civilization is repeated to a certain extent in the primeval Indian civilization.

When we consider the successive civilizations of the post-Atlantean epoch, we can see that they represent successive recapitulations of conditions experienced earlier in the physical body, but which have been transformed through the forces of rejuvenation. Thus the Persian civilization shows a conflict between the virile forces of early manhood, when man is still subject to the influences of the abnormal Spirits of Form, and the forces which stem from the normal Spirits of Form. In the Persian civilization this dualism is reflected in the polarity of light and darkness, of Ormuzd and Ahriman.

The farther we move westward the more we see that the civilization bears the impress of the characteristics of a more mature age. We must admit that up to the present time the creations of man are still dependent to a large extent upon the abnormal forces and Beings of the universe. Nevertheless we can now understand that racial characteristics are no longer decisive factors as man moves westward and also that, to a certain extent, the tendency of civilization is such that its youthful vigour, its creative potentialities, decline more and more the further it moves towards the West.

To the unprejudiced observer a variety of factors serves to show that our contemporary civilization is also determined in this way in accordance with a fixed law. But people are not disposed to be objective. If you bear in mind that, in reality, all civilization is in a state of flux, you will then realize that the further we move westward, the less productive civilization becomes. As civilization it is already moribund. The further West one goes, the more civilization becomes externalized; it is no longer vitalized by the forces of youth, but is given over to the hardening forces of old age. Western man will still be able to benefit mankind by making valuable and important contributions in physics, chemistry and astronomy and in all fields which are independent of the rejuvenating forces of youth. But that which calls for creative energy requires a different configuration of those forces which work upon man.

Let us take the example of a man growing up from childhood to the stage when his spiritual life matures. He first develops physically. The forces concentrated within the youthful organism must be allowed to expand physically. Later, when growth is completed, these physical forces are turned inwards. Mankind in general undergoes a similar process. The curve of development which we have already described reveals a remarkable law which applies even to the continents. First of all we observe the first signs of man's development in Africa; then his native territory expands far afield. Characteristic of this expansion are the wide open spaces of Asia where man inhabits vast tracts of country.

Let us now glance at the repetition of race development in the post-Atlantean civilizations. Just as in his youth man looks out with curiosity upon his environment, so does the man of the old Indian civilization look out into the world. This is associated

with the fresh, youthful forces which help man to grow until he
reaches his full stature when the spiritual life must begin to
unfold and the physical must be compressed. As civilization ad-
vances westward into Europe it is remarkable that the geographical area which mankind inhabits is narrowed down to
smaller and smaller lands. We observe that Europe is the smallest
continent, and the further civilization moves westward the more
it tends towards delimitation, and finally in its westward course
is confined to peninsulas and islands.

All this is connected with the spiritual course of evolution.
Here we have a unique insight into the mysteries of spiritual
evolution. But with this narrowing of the geographical area a
critical situation arises; on account of this crisis a more unpro-
ductive element begins to operate. Creative activity dies out to
some extent in the peninsulas the further westward one goes.
This creative impoverishment is illustrated in what I have
already described, namely that civilization itself, the further it
moves westward, becomes progressively more rigid and senile,
and slowly declines. This was always known in the Mystery
Schools. You will now understand why I said that what I had to
communicate might be somewhat dangerous because people
might take offence. By no means everything can be revealed that
would enable man to command the higher members of his being
so that he may perceive the terrestrial forces that determine the
race, forces that later on determine the character of the civilization and which in a still later epoch will have lost their significance when man rediscovers his spiritual vision. Thus you will
understand that the whole process of the evolution of mankind is
connected with the spiritual evolution which has always been
known to those who were initiated into the deeper secrets of
existence. The truth of what I have just said does not depend
upon whether one approves or disapproves; it depends upon
evolutionary necessity. To deny this necessity is pointless; it
serves only to put obstacles in the way of understanding. Therefore it is only natural that those who migrate to areas lying more
to the West must seek rejuvenating power, spiritual substance,
from the East; but Central Europe must call to mind its own
creative activity as it existed before the formation of peninsulas

and islands. That is why precisely in Europe—in the region embracing our two countries, Scandinavia and Germany—man has to draw upon the resources of his own soul-life and why, on the other hand, we must look especially in the West for that part of humanity which is to receive spiritual nourishment from the East. This urge is deeply rooted in the nature of all mankind. You see this repeated in the development of Spiritual Science. We witness it again in the fourth post-Atlantean civilization, amongst the Greeks and Romans. The Romans, it is true, are in certain respects more advanced than the Greeks, but they took their spiritual life from the people they conquered, who lived more towards the East.

The further countries lie to the West the more is the law thus revealed to us confirmed. Now these important truths can only be indicated; they reveal what accords with the inner nature of the future mission of mankind in every corner of the globe. We must understand therefore the task that lies before us if we wish to raise ourselves to the level of the all-human. Here lies the great responsibility which we take upon ourselves if we wish to participate in the spiritual evolution of mankind. In this realm neither personal sympathy nor personal enthusiasm may play a part. They are of no consequence; only what is determined by the great laws of humanity is decisive. The great laws themselves must apprise us of this; we must not allow ourselves to be prejudiced in favour of any particular law.

That is the fundamental characteristic of Rosicrucianism. Rosicrucianism implies acting in accordance with the evolution of all mankind. If we are aware of the configuration of the landscape we inhabit, including islands and peninsulas, then we shall realize what sentiments must fill our hearts if we seek to work for the benefit of the evolution of humanity.

In the remote past man descended to Earth under the guidance of the abnormal Spirits of Form and was associated with his particular geographical region. Thus the foundations were laid for the development of the races. Then a progressive intermingling of the races takes place. The evolution of races is interrupted to make way for the evolution of nations, i.e. nations develop out of races. And the development of nations enters even into the evolution of the individual human being. Behind the question, who was Plato, what was his origin and ancestry—a great mystery is concealed. He was an individual who grew up in the lineage of Solon, was a member of the Ionian tribe, the Greek nation and the whole Caucasian race. The realization that Plato was a descendant of Solon, an Ionian, a Greek, a Caucasian, expresses a profound mystery if we understand the law behind it. It shows us how the normal and abnormal Spirits of Form whose major concern is to prepare man's incarnation on Earth work in concert over the whole Earth, how, by this cooperative activity, the human race is subdivided and how then those other Beings intervene of whom we have already spoken when describing the characteristics of the several peoples. Each individual is intimately associated with these processes by means of which all these higher Beings, these higher Spirits, determine the evolution of the world by their cooperative activity.

We cannot understand the individual if we do not see how he owes his whole development to the cooperation of these Beings. Because a Caucasian race was once created on Earth through the mysterious interplay of the normal and abnormal Spirits of Form the stage was set for the incarnation of a Plato. And because we are aware of the intervention of the normal and abnormal Archangels down to the Angels, we realize the steps which were necessary to bring forth a Plato whom we could recognize as a human being endowed with the specific human attributes of thinking, feeling and willing. The nation occupies an intermediate position between the race and the individual.

It was first necessary therefore to outline the conditions fundamental to the evolution of race. Tomorrow we shall discuss the emergence of nations out of races, the intervention of other Spirits of the Hierarchies and especially their intervention in the activity of the Spirits of Form.

LECTURE FIVE

Manifestation of the Hierarchies in the Elements of Nature. The Mission of the planetary Epochs of Old Saturn, Old Sun, Old Moon and Earth.

It will be seen from the last lecture that if we wish to make an impartial study of the facts underlying our present investigation we must transcend those prejudices which might easily arise on matters which I must now describe objectively. So long as one has the slightest tendency to take personally an objective description of a particular race or people, it will be difficult to reach an unprejudiced understanding of the facts presented in this lecture-course. For this reason these matters can only be discussed in the light of Spiritual Science. For however deeply one may be involved emotionally in a particular people or race, as Anthroposophists we have an adequate counterpoise in the teaching of karma and reincarnation, when rightly understood. This teaching opens a vista into the future and reveals that our integral Self is incarnated in successive ages in different races and peoples. When we contemplate the destiny of our integral Self we may be sure that we shall share not only the positive or perhaps also the negative aspects of all races and peoples; but we may be sure that in our inmost being we shall also receive the countless blessings of all races and all peoples since we are incarnated in different races at different times.

Our consciousness, our horizon, is enlarged through these ideas of karma and reincarnation. Only through these teachings therefore do we learn to accept what is revealed to us at the present time concerning the mysterious relations of race and nation. If we rightly understand the theme of these lectures we shall harbour no regrets at having incarnated in a particular people or race. But an objective survey of national and racial characteristics may, nonetheless, provoke dissension and disharmony unless it is accepted in the spirit I have already sugges-

ted. The aspirant for spiritual knowledge will learn through the
teachings of karma and reincarnation how every nation, even
the smallest nation, has to contribute its share towards the total
evolution of humanity. In the second part of this lecture-course
I propose to show—and herein lies its real importance—how the
particular influences of the missions of the several peoples are
merged in the whole of humanity and how even isolated ethnic
groups which are scattered here and there amongst larger
national groups have their part to play in the great harmony of
human evolution. This, however, will only become apparent to
us step by step.

In order to acquire a full understanding of the characteristics
of the individual Folk Souls we shall have to select examples
which are clearer to us in certain respects than the folk characteristics of our own times. On the other hand, we shall perhaps have
to deal with folk characteristics which belong to a more distant
epoch, in order to have a yard-stick for determining the characteristics and tasks of the different nations. But this will be nothing
more than a general outline of the racial or folk characteristics.

In the course of the last lectures we have learned that a race
is the product of the cooperative activity of a normal and abnormal Spirit of Form, and a people the product of a normal and
abnormal Archangel; and we now understand how the Beings
of the spiritual Hierarchies intervene in evolution.

The question now arises; how do the Beings of a higher order
work into the external world? It would be as well to begin by
acquiring today an understanding of the Hierarchies of which
man is the lowest member. You will recall that we placed man
on the lowest rung of the Hierarchical ladder. Below him are the
three kingdoms of nature, the animal, vegetable and mineral kingdoms. Above him are the Angels, the Archangels and the Archai
or First Beginnings. This is the Hierarchy immediately above
man—the third Hierarchy. The second Hierarchy is as
follows:

> Spirits of Form—Powers (Exusiai)
> Spirits of Movement—Mights (Dynamis)
> Spirits of Wisdom—Dominions (Kyriotetes)

Then we have the highest of the three Hierarchies—the first Hierarchy:

Spirits of Will—Thrones
Cherubim
Seraphim

Since all spiritual Beings manifest in some form or other and are to be found therefore in the phenomenal world, the realm of Maya or illusion, we must ask ourselves where we must look for them at the lowest stage of manifestation, at the stage of illusion. In his normal perception of Nature and the Spirit man knows only the realm of Maya, the most external manifestation of these spiritual Beings. I propose to illustrate this by means of an example.

Let us suppose a person is travelling on foot over the bare, rugged landscape of Norway. His first impression will be of a rocky expanse spread out before him. He will describe this solid rock formation in terms of his first impression, namely as hard "rocky substance". But he who penetrates into the being of natural pnenomena has a totally different conception of this "rocky substance". What is the real nature of that upon which we stand and which offers resistance? The external surface of the Earth which man believes to have a real existence does not exist at all, it is an illusion. In reality spiritual forces are at work radiating from below, from within the Earth; they emanate from certain Beings. Thus in a particular locality we see a manifestation of forces emanating from the Earth and raying outward in all directions. But if these forces alone were present, clearly man would not have solid ground under his feet, for of themselves they would project him with maximum velocity into space. He owes his ability to stand on solid ground to the circumstance that other forces stream in from all sides from universal space. Where the forces streaming in from the Universe encounter the forces raying outward from within the Earth there arises, so to speak, a frontier or boundary which is the apparent surface of the Earth. The surface one sees, therefore, is only an illusion; it is a result of the activity of the in-streaming and outward streaming forces which neutralize each other at the apparent surface in question.

The forces raying outward in all directions are the forces of the Thrones, the Spirits of Will. The forces streaming in from the Universe are essentially the forces that proceed from the Spirits of Movement. Thus these two forces meet at this frontier and this interplay of the Thrones with the Spirits of Movement—since the activity of the Thrones is neutralized by the Spirits of Movement—produces the diversified contours of the Earth's surface. What is seen externally as the Earth's surface is wholly unreal; it is simply illusion. In reality it is the product of a balance of forces; an agreement, as it were, is concluded between the Spirits of Will and the Spirits of Movement as a consequence of which the Earth assumes its highly diversified configurations.

Nevertheless through this interplay alone our Earth could not arrive at its present planetary form. The forces of the Spirits of Will and the Spirits of Movement acting and reacting upon each other would not be sufficient for this; the resultant effect would be something totally different. If, for example, only the Spirits of Will were to *ray outwards* from within the Earth and were opposed by the Spirits of Movement alone, then the Earth would be in a continual state of flux, the ever moving forms could not be brought to rest. In that event, it is true, it would not be as fluid as the ocean in its present state; it would not be of a liquid consistency like water that is ruffled at the slightest breath of wind, but of a viscous, semi-fluid consistency.

If you wish to form an idea of how the Spirits of Will and the Spirits of Movement originally worked in concert, I would like to give you an example and would ask you to follow me on the sketch. In the first place let me draw your attention to the Alps which today form a solid mountain chain so that the solid barrier of the Alpine Massif divides the Italian peninsula in the South from the rest of Europe. How is one to account for this Alpine chain? There was a time in the far distant past when the Alpine Massif did not as yet exist, but to the North and West there were already older eminencies which at that time had already become solidified. Waves of semi-fluid consistency were then thrown up from the South. We may picture the situation somewhat as follows:

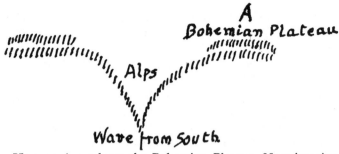

Here at A we have the Bohemian Plateau. Now imagine a huge wave thrown up from the South which divided and spilled over the Bohemian Plateau on the right (to the East) and over the central plateau of France on the left (to the West). In primeval times this mighty wave formed the Alpine Massif. It is possible to arrive at this conclusion without specialist knowledge. Anyone who has once stood on the summit of one of the Alpine peaks and surveyed the unique configuration of the Alpine chain has observed—even if he were unaware of it—what Spiritual Science has long established and which even the present-day geologists have confirmed—that peculiar wave-like formation which dates from the time when the primeval mass of the Earth was still in a semi-fluid condition.

Such would be the configuration of the Earth today through the cooperation of the Spirits of Will and the Spirits of Movement but for the intervention of another activity which is remarkably persistent and which is manifested on the surface of our Earth by the interweaving of the activity of the Spirits of Form with the Spirits of Will (the Thrones) who work in conjunction with the Spirits of Movement. You may picture therefore that these Spirits of Form, dancing as it were upon the waves, brought the ever-moving forms to rest and moulded them into form. We can therefore point to the cooperative activity on the part of three different forces which proceed from three kinds of Beings. On the one hand we see the activity of the Spirits of Form who work inward from the cosmic sphere and unfold their activity in the realms of the Spirits of Will below them as well as in that of the Spirits of Movement above them. That which on our Earth appears externally for the most part as a fluid element

—not the liquid water we see around us today, but the primal semi-fluid element which was brought to rest by the Spirits of Form—this we must look upon as the most external manifestation of the Spirits of Will. But another element is always associated with this activity. The Spirits of Will (or Thrones) are assisted by the Cherubim or Seraphim. The Cherubim work in the air element, in everything aeriform which permeates the apparent solid substance of the Earth. Air is an illusion behind which stand the mighty Beings we call Cherubim. The Seraphim work in fire, they operate in whatsoever manifests as heat.

Thus we see how the radiations from the centre influence our Earth planet. Our planet therefore is so constituted that the Spirits of Will (or Thrones), the Seraphim and the Cherubim work from the centre. We must look upon our planet in this way: at the meeting-place of the boundaries of air and heat or warmth —for the atmosphere is just as much part of our planet as the water or dry land—a surface is formed. Upon this surface the Spirits of Form literally dance upon the waves and bring them to rest and mould them into form. It was for this reason that they were given their name. Behind them are the Spirits of Movement and in their element again is mingled what we called the Spirits of Wisdom. When therefore we look inward towards the centre of our planet we are aware of the presence of Divine Beings, Thrones, Cherubim and Seraphim. When we look outward we perceive first of all beyond the realm of the Spirits of Form who permeate the air and heat with their element, the Spirits of Movement and the Spirits of Wisdom. When we gaze out into the periphery of the Earth, when we lift our eyes to the Cosmic Spheres, all the nature-forces and natural phenomena we encounter there are fundamentally the work of the second Hierarchy. Everything we see when we look into the depths of the Earth we ascribe to the Beings of the first (highest) Hierarchy. It is to the unique cooperative activity of these two Hierarchies that we owe the configuration of our environment.

We have stated that the three elements, water, air and fire are related to the Spirits of Will, the Cherubim and Seraphim. In which of these elements do the Spirits of Form manifest themselves? They are the Beings nearest to us and they "dance upon"

the surface of the Earth where we live and have our being. They
work inward from universal space, but now unfold their forces
in the emanations issuing from the Earth. To us they are concentrated in the rays of the Sun. Light, therefore, is the element in
which the Spirits of Form first weave and work. Since, however,
the activities of light and everything related thereunto manifest
themselves at the frontier where the Spirits of Movement and
Spirits of Will work in concert, it is at this meeting-place that
solid forms are created. Man has, at first, no organs which would
enable him to see what lies beyond these forces of light which we
call the Spirits of Form, no organs with which to preceive that
which is woven into the light. Everything which on our Earth
determines creation and destruction, all the chemical forces
active in the Earth, is still interwoven with light and this is
principally the domain in which the Spirits of Movement
operate. When man learns to perceive something of that which
he otherwise looks upon simply as Maya, in the action of chemical
synthesis and analysis, then he hears these Spirits of Movement, he
perceives the Music of the Spheres of which the Pythagorean and
other occult schools speak. That too is what Goethe describes when
he speaks of the Sun, not as the giver of light, but when he says:

> The Sun, in ancient guise, competing
> With brother spheres in rival song,
> With thunder-march, his orb completing
> Moves his predestin'd course along.
> > (*Faust.* Prologue in Heaven.
> > Tr. Anna Swanwick)

This Music of the Spheres is still there, but it is inaudible to
ordinary consciousness. It is a reality, it approaches all men
from without as an astral effect. Man, however, does not hear it.
If in relation to this he were to experience an alternation similar to
that of light and dark at certain times, then there would also be
times when he could hear the Music of the Spheres. It sounds forth
both day and night and therefore he can only hear it if he undergoes a certain occult training and development. Whereas the light
streams towards us during the day as light and during the night
continues to operate as a reservoir of assimilated light, the Music

of the Spheres sounds forth continually both day and night. In this situation man is in the same position as the miller who is aware of the sound of his mill-wheel only when it is no longer working.

The last of the Beings of the Second Hierarchy are the Spirits of Wisdom, who work from the surrounding Cosmos into the weaving light and into the Music of the Spheres operating throughout the Universe. That is the Life of the universal Ether, raying in on to the Earth. For Life is pouring in on to the Earth from cosmic spaces and is received by living creatures here on Earth. It comes from the Spirits of Wisdom.

Thus we gaze out into cosmic spaces and perceive first of all the Sun in which these threefold forces are concentrated for our spiritual vision. We perceive how *instreaming Life, weaving Sound, formative Light,* the trinity of the second Hierarchy, are working in from universal space. The highest of the Hierarchies, the Seraphim, the Cherubim and the Thrones, work upwards from below, from the centre of the Earth. The third Hierarchy (the Hierarchy immediately above man) is interwoven with all terrestrial activity and works chiefly in the inner being of organic life. To this Hierarchy belong, in the first place, the Archai acting as the Time Spirits. These Time Spirits work in the material prepared for them by the higher Hierarchies; they lay the foundation of what we call the history of mankind, the evolution of civilization on Earth. Then in our immediate environment we find the Archangels, the tribal Folk Spirits, and finally the Angels who mediate between the individual human beings and the Archangels.

To sum up, therefore: In the forces of Nature upon our planet, in earth, water, air and fire are the Beings of the first or highest Hierarchy who stream forth to meet the activity of the Spirits of Form working in from the cosmic sphere. From outside, the Beings of the second Hierarchy stream in, and in the environment of the Earth are the Beings of the third Hierarchy who, for the moment, are the weakest of the forces. Just imagine for a moment how powerful are the forces of those exalted Beings whom we call the Spirits of Will, who fashion the very ground under our feet. Then we have those forces which stream in from outside, the Spirits of Form who are nearest to us, and who

mould the contours of the Earth in their plastic state. And finally
we have Angels, Archangels and Archai who work more intimately into human souls. And so in the first (highest) Hierarchy
we have those forces of Nature which we recognize as the strongest—the Nature-forces emanating from the centre of the Earth,
the forces of the solid Earth beneath us. In the second Hierarchy
we have the cosmic forces which live and weave around us in the
ether and in the third Hierarchy we have that which lives and
weaves in the inner recesses of our soul.

If we observe the cooperative activity of these three Hierarchies and see how they operate in our Earth planet, how they
form it out of the totality of the Universe, then we have some
indication of what was necessary in order to create our Earth.
The Earth had to pass through the planetary epochs of Old
Saturn, Old Sun, and Old Moon before it could become our
present Earth. If you refer to my books *Cosmic Memory* and
Occult Science you will find that, even during the earlier incarnations of our Earth, these various spiritual Beings worked
together, but that the nature of this cooperative activity was
different from that of today. With each new incarnation in the
Saturn, Sun, Moon and Earth states the cooperative activity of
those Hierarchical Beings assumed a different form because
in each of these planetary epochs of the Earth the Hierarchical
Beings had their specific task to fulfil. We may confidently
affirm that each of the conditions through which our Earth
has passed and those which still lie before it, represent, and have
represented, a particular stage in the process of cosmic evolution.

Since all conceptions change from one planetary condition to
another it is extremely difficult to define what were the tasks
of the Old Saturn, Old Sun and Old Moon epochs. This is
not easy because we must first characterize the mission of our
Earth in a very general way. The simplest way to conceive of it is
to call to mind the nature of the various forces which manifest
themselves in space. Man's inner life consists of thinking, feeling
and willing; his outer vehicles consist of the physical body,
etheric body and astral body. So that if we take a man of the
present day and ignore for the moment his ego, we can envisage
him as a tapestry consisting of the physical, etheric and astral

bodies into which are woven—as into an outer envelope—
thinking, feeling and willing.

Now these forces in man, both in the outer and the inner man,
are always related to some earlier mission which was connected
with a former incarnation of the Earth. If, for example, we wish
to form an approximate idea of the Saturn mission, we may think
of it as being related, on the one hand, to the human physical
body and, on the other, to the human will. Now if there had been
no Saturn incarnation of our Earth, neither the life of will in
man, nor his physical body could have attained their present
form. A man owes his physical body and life of will to Old
Saturn. He is indebted to the Akashic Records for this knowledge.
The after-effects of each Earth incarnation, however, are reflected
in the forms of the succeeding incarnations. Hence the life of will
as we know it today can be traced back to the after-effects of the
Saturn element. Consequently the Saturn element is reflected
in the inner life of man as *will*. You will have an idea of the
mission of the Old Sun epoch if you study the etheric body and
also the later development of the sentient life. You already know
that the etheric body can be traced back to the Old Sun. The
after-effects however are such that man was able to develop
later the inner life of feeling. Finally, we find that the Old Moon
condition was related to the astral body of man and the inner life
of thought. Thus three successive incarnations of the Earth were
necessary in order that these forces of the inner and outer man—
physical body, etheric body and astral body; thinking, feeling
and willing—could so develop that they are now an integral
part of his physical and spiritual life. In order that the task of the
three successive incarnations or planetary epochs of our Earth
could be fulfilled and that man could be endowed with his
present constitutional make-up, those Beings whom we have
described as belonging to the Hierarchies were obliged to work
together in each of these planetary epochs in a way appropriate
to each Earth incarnation.

The mission of Old Saturn therefore had to be fulfilled,
otherwise man's physical body and the life of will could not have
been bestowed upon him. To the Old Sun he owed his etheric
body and sentient life, and finally to the Old Moon he owed the

astral body and the power of thought. Thus, each of the three preceding incarnations of our Earth were especially devoted to one of the salient aspects of our individual being, our 'I'. In effect the external physical body which stems from the activity of the Spiritual Beings of Old Saturn, from the Spirits of Will, is simply Will that is externalized. Today the will is an expression of the inner life. These words are carefully chosen; they are no flight of fancy, but fit the facts completely. You can learn much from them. The Earth passed through the Old Sun epoch in order, on the one hand, to lay the foundation of the etheric body through the influence of the Spirits of Wisdom, and, on the other hand, through the continued operation of the element of wisdom, to endow us inwardly with Feeling, the inner element of Wisdom. The mission of Old Moon is associated with the astral body and the inner life of Thought.

The problem which now confronts us is this: what particular mission has been chosen by the Spirits of Form who work chiefly on the Earth and fashion it?

Now the task before the Spirits of Will or Thrones who worked chiefly on Old Saturn was to endow man with that element which later, during Earth-evolution, manifests itself as Will. The great task of Old Saturn, then, is to implant the will, the forces of will. When we contemplate this gift to man, we are filled with admiration and reverence for the ruling cosmic Powers. They command our deep respect when we realize that for the skilful interweaving of outer Will, which resides in our physical body, and of inner Will, a special planetary mission was necessary. The whole world of the Hierarchies had to suffer the birth and death of a planet in order to bring about the condition which we experience as the outer and inner element of Will. In the same way, the Old Sun universe was necessary in order to endow us with the etheric body and the element of Feeling, the inner element of Wisdom. And the Old Moon mission was necessary in order to endow us with the astral body and the inner life of Thought. What, then, is the mission of the Spirits of Form? What is the real Mission of the Earth? If one associates the Old Saturn mission with the endowment of the element of Will, the Old Sun mission principally with the endowment of the

element of Feeling, and the Moon mission chiefly with that of
the element of Thought—with the astral body of man—then the
mission of the Earth is to bring about a perfect harmony between
these three elements, each of which had been predominant in an
earlier incarnation of our Earth. The mission of our Earth is to
resolve the conflict between these elements and restore a proper
harmony between them. Man is involved in this mission of the
Earth in order that he may establish this harmony between
thinking, feeling and willing, first of all in his own inner being.
At the beginning of the Earth period man was in this respect a
patchwork of thought, feeling and will. Everyone who possesses a
little self-knowledge can feel that the man of today has not yet
achieved inner harmony; he is frequently a victim of conflict and
discord. Man is called upon first of all to strike a balance between
thought, feeling and will within himself by means of which he
himself as an Ego-being can demonstrate and communicate to
his fellow men what this harmony signifies.

In occult symbolism this Earth-mission has always been
expressed in a special way by means of a geometrical figure.
Amongst geometrical figures you will find none which corresponds so exactly to the balance or harmony of these three
activities as the equilateral triangle. If you draw an equilateral
triangle you will find the three sides are equal, the three angles
equal, the vertices are equidistant from each other and all are
equidistant from the centre. The centre of an equilateral triangle is
a complete symbol of a balance of forces, so that when the occultist looks at an equilateral triangle he perceives in it a symbol
of the perfectly balanced cooperation of those elements, each of
which held for a time the upper hand in the three earlier incarnations of our Earth. The deeds of the 'I' in man signify simply the
creation of an active centre in his nature whereby this state of
harmony can be prepared from within. Man therefore is called to
high destiny on Earth to bring about from within, first of all through
his whole being, a balance between what was predominant for a
time in earlier planetary epochs in various ways and at various times.

Now that is a very general definition of our Earth mission, but
this mission is exactly as I have described it. The secret of this
mission is that through this cooperation, through this balance or

harmony of the three forces, the inner being really creates something new. A fourth element which is the element of Love is thus
added to the three preceding elements. Love can only develop in
the busy work-a-day world when an absolute harmony exists
between the three forces which in earlier epochs were each in turn
the dominating influence. We shall have more to say about this
in the next few days. For the moment you must accept it as a
general description.

Thus our planet is the planet of Love and therefore the result of
this balance or harmony which is reflected in the cooperation
of the three forces is the active spirit of Love, and this spirit
of Love is to be woven into the whole of evolution throughout all
the successive incarnations of the Earth by the fulfilment of the
Earth's mission. In this way the Trinity becomes a Quaternary:
the latter begins with its fourth element at the lowest stage, with
the most elementary or primitive form of love which is so purged
and purified that at the close of the Earth-evolution Love will
appear as an element enjoying to the full equal status with the
others. To fulfil the mission of balance or harmony ordained for
our Earth planet implies, in reality, transforming the Trinity into
a Quaternary. To make the Trinity into a Quaternary is therefore
an occult formula for the Earth's secret. Inevitably the fourth
element is today still very imperfect. But when the Earth shall
have fulfilled its mission, it will appear as luminous as the
Sacred Triangle which, with its state of perfect balance, shines
forth as the highest symbol we possess for our Earth-ideal in so far
as we can remember the past of the Earth.

This correspondence between the elements of thinking, feeling
and willing is such that the inmost being of man becomes the
substance of Love and this is what one may call the really creative,
the inwardly creative element in earthly existence. We must
therefore describe the Spirits of Form in their totality (because
their particular mission is to harmonize the three former conditions) as the Spirits of Love.

In considering Earth-existence in this way we first described
thinking, feeling and willing and the working of Love outside our
Earth planet and we described as the special task of the Spirits
of Form the implanting of Love which results from balance or

harmony. This is the whole mission of the Earth. In order to realize this power of Love that shall permeate the Earth, the interplay and interaction of the lowest Hierarchies was necessary. As we began to indicate in our previous study, the network of Love must be woven by these Hierarchies and Love must be woven in such a way that the principal threads are woven by the normal Spirits of Form, for that is their fundamental mission. Then the abnormal Spirits of Form, who are in reality Spirits of Movement, weave into the tapestry that which creates the different races. Then the normal and abnormal Time Spirits weave into it the historical evolution, and the normal and abnormal Archangels the evolution of the individual peoples and languages; and finally the Angels who determine man's rightful place on Earth participate in this activity. In this way the mighty tapestry of Love is being woven. Yet of this tapestry of Love which is being woven as the real mission of Earth only the Maya, the outer reflection, is visible on Earth.

The nearest realm above the physical world in which it is possible to perceive this tapestry is the astral world. In order to see the working of the Hierarchies more and more clearly in the truths underlying our external Maya we must raise our consciousness from the astral plane to the planes of lower and higher Devachan. We then perceive how this tapestry is woven. If we raise our consciousness to the astral plane, the Beings normally working from the depths, namely, the Spirits of Will (Thrones), Cherubim and Seraphim are not yet visible. If we wish to perceive these Spirits at work we must raise our spiritual vision to still higher realms. But already in the astral world we find the abnormal Spirits of Form who, if they had fulfilled their normal evolution, would be working from without. The Spirits of the second Hierarchy, as we already know, ought to work from without, from the celestial spheres, but here they are working from within, from the centre of the Earth. Thus into this tapestry of Love in which the Spirits of Movement, the Spirits of Form and the Spirits of Wisdom are working from without, and the Spirits of Will, the Seraphim and Cherubim from within, there are also other Beings working from within who should really be working from without. They work secretly, however, after the manner in which the silkworm spins its cocoon. What is seen first of all in the astral world are Beings working from the depths. These singular Spirits of Movement who have transposed their sphere and are fallen Spirits, are the first Beings to become visible amongst those spiritual Beings weaving and surging in the spiritual atmosphere of the Earth. These Beings who are the first to become visible on the astral plane, even before the normal Angels, are the Spirits who in a sense falsify clairvoyant perception—despite the fact that they are vitally necessary for the propagation of the races. These Spirits, each of whom has many attendant spirits, because each one begets many spiritually subordinate beings, are surrounded in the spiritual world by a number of spiritual beings who are always subordinate to their respective Hierarchies. The higher Spirits also have their attendant Nature-spirits—the Spirits of Will: the Undines; the Cherubim: the Sylphs; the Seraphim: the Salamanders. The abnormal Spirits of Form who are really Spirits of Movement and who appear as hideous spiritual Beings on the astral plane also have their subordinate spirits. They are the spirits who are actively engaged in whatsoever is associated with the genesis of the human races, in that which in man is associated with the earth-bound, with the propagation of race and the like. These beings, indeed this whole domain is one of the most variegated and dangerous of the astral world and—this is the appropriate moment to call attention to it—it is the one most easily contacted by those who attain to clairvoyant vision by erroneous methods. The hosts of these spirits who are associated with the propagation of the race, who serve that purpose, are those most easily perceived. Many a one who has entered into the occult realm prematurely or in the wrong way has had to pay dearly for it because he encountered this host of spiritual beings without the harmonizing influence of the other spiritual Beings.

Thus we have been able to throw light upon that which weaves on the loom of Reality in order to produce this tapestry from which the pattern of man's psychic life emerges. Tomorrow we will discuss in further detail how this cosmic pattern which we have touched upon today is reflected in the origin and development of races and peoples.

LECTURE SIX

The five Root Races of Mankind.

It is a very complicated matter, as you may well imagine, when the Spirits of the different Hierarchies have to coordinate their forces in such a way that the mission of the Earth can be fulfilled and ultimately a state of balance or equilibrium be achieved. You will understand therefore that statements such as those made in our last lecture are valid only in so far as they refer to a definite period in evolution and that the whole picture changes immediately one depicts evolution at another period. Hence in order to arrive at a fuller understanding of these complex problems a particular course of lectures cannot be isolated from the rest.

I shall here draw attention to one point only and what I am about to say is to be taken as footnote or addendum to the lectures on the Spiritual Hierarchies.* In creating the harmony or equilibrium of our Earth the whole cooperation of the Hierarchies is involved and we must envisage the Spirits of Will, the Cherubim and Seraphim, which we described yesterday as the highest Hierarchy, as raying outward from the Earth. We must envisage these Beings as originally working inward from the Universe towards the centre of the Earth. Man does not become aware of these forces in the former aspect but only in the latter aspect when they are reflected from the Earth's centre.

You will only be able, therefore, to form a complete picture of the very intimate processes which here take place if you compare what was said in my last lecture with the more detailed information about the Hierarchies in the lecture-course given at

*This lecture-course was given in Düsseldorf, in April 1909, and was entitled: *Spiritual Hierarchies and their Reflection in the physical World. Zodiac, Planets, Cosmos.*

Düsseldorf, in which a comprehensive picture was given of the cosmic activity of the three Hierarchies. These things are by no means so simple, and in order to make the mission of the Earth comprehensible we must approach this problem in such a way that we are prepared to accept that the Spirits of these Hierarchies are reflected in the elements of Earth existence. If you bear this in mind then you will also sense the infinite wisdom inherent in a universe of relationships. To a certain extent you will also feel that the field of knowledge must be continually enlarged, that it is unlimited, since things are so complicated that when we imagine we have grasped one point of view we immediately reject it in favour of another which throws light on the problem from a different angle. We can only advance step by step in our knowledge: Nevertheless from the indications given in the last lecture, especially at the close of that lecture, you will have a clearer understanding of the cooperation between the normal and abnormal Spirits of Form, a cooperation which ensures that the population of the Earth should not be limited to a single homogeneous species spread over the whole Earth, but that a diversity of individual races should be possible. In order to achieve that corporate humanity which is only possible to man in the course of Earth-evolution, it would have been necessary for the normal Spirits of Form to act independently. These are the same spiritual Beings who in Genesis are called the Elohim. In the whole Universe which surrounds the Earth and together with the Earth forms a single whole, we can distinguish seven of these normal Spirits of Form. There are therefore seven Spirits of Form or seven Elohim. If we wish to form a conception of these seven Elohim with their various missions and their task of establishing Harmony or Love as the ultimate mission of the Earth, we must clearly understand that these seven Spirits of Form cooperate in such a way that what we described in Lecture Four as "man in the second third of his life" would become a reality. Thus, if all these seven Spirits of Form could work in accordance with their declared intention, then collectively they would fashion the real Ego-being. But as other spiritual Beings cooperate with them and diversify this uniform humanity, it was found necessary to make special preparations in the Cosmos. If today you wish to find in the Cosmos the sphere of activity of the normal Spirits of Form—those Beings who, as I described yesterday, shine down upon us in the light from our present Cosmos—then you must seek for them in the Sun. You must always look towards the Sun sphere for that cosmic "Lodge", that community in the Universe, where these Spirits of Form plan to establish the earthly harmony and to fulfil the mission of Earth-evolution. Lest the activity of the abnormal Spirits of Form should provoke too great a disharmony amongst mankind, one of the Spirits had to detach Himself from the community. In reality, therefore, only six Spirits of Form or Elohim work from the Sun; one of these Spirits had to detach Himself lest the simultaneous activity of the abnormal Spirits of Form, who are really Spirits of Movement should disturb the balance or harmony. It was the Spirit who in the Bible, in Genesis, is called Jahve or Jehovah. If you wish to follow His activity in the Universe you must look for it, not in the Sun sphere, but in the Moon sphere at a particular epoch. I have touched upon this in my *Occult Science—an Outline* from another angle, where I have shown that the Spirits of Form withdraw with the separation of the Sun, but in the special disposition following upon the separation of the Moon, the preliminary conditions were first established for the further evolution of man. For if the Moon had remained united with the Earth the evolution of man could not have taken place. This further evolution of man has only been made possible because one of the Elohim, Jahve, accompanied the separation of the Moon— while the other six Spirits remained in the Sun—and because Jahve cooperated with His six colleagues to counteract the forces of the backward Spirits of Movement.

Now the separation of the Sun was a necessity for the following reasons: after certain older Spirits of Movement who possessed more potent forces than the Spirits of Form—for they stand higher in the rank of the Hierarchies—had decided to remain behind, the normal Spirits of Form were obliged to modify their activity by detaching one of their members, otherwise they would not have been able to establish the balance or harmony necessary for further evolution.

If we wish to have a clear idea of the activities of these normal

Spirits of Form it is best to think of them as streaming down to us in the sunlight. If, however, we wish to understand how the abnormal Spirits of Form cooperate with the normal Spirits of Form who are centred in the Sun (for Jahve withdrew towards the Moon sphere solely for the purpose of establishing the equilibrium), then we must imagine that a certain Sun-force, which streams towards us in the normal Spirits of Form is modified by the force that rays down to us from the abnormal Spirits of Form who are really Spirits of Movement. These have their centre in the other five planets, in Saturn, Jupiter, Mars, Venus and Mercury, speaking in terms of the seven heavenly bodies of ancient astronomy.

When you look out into the Cosmos you have now a picture of the distribution of the normal and abnormal Spirits of Form. Six of the normal Spirits of Form are centred in the Sun and one of them, Jahve or Jehovah, from the sphere of the Moon acts as a counterpoise by virtue of His function as Regent and Guide of that sphere. The activities of these Spirits of Form are influenced by the activities proceeding from Saturn, Jupiter, Mars, Venus and Mercury. The forces of the abnormal Spirits stream down upon the Earth, are arrested by the Earth and ray outward again from the Earth-centre as was described at the close of the last lecture.

Thus if the Elohim or normal Spirits of Form, operating from the Sun, are active in a particular region of the Earth's surface, then only the normal 'I', that which determines man's normal being, his general make-up, would come into existence in that particular region. Now the forces of Mercury, for example, mingle with these forces of the normal Spirits of Form which, but for the state of equilibrium, would "dance" upon the surface of the Earth. Hence in that which here manifests in the potent forces of the Spirits of Form, there dance and vibrate not only the normal forces but also that which intermingles with the normal forces of the Elohim or Spirits of Form, namely that which emanates from the abnormal Spirits of Form who are centred in the several planets. Thus we see that through these abnormal Spirits of Form there are five potential centres of influence where these reflected planetary forces are concentrated and produce in effect what we know as the five Root Races of the Earth.

Let us now look more closely into the centre which, in Lecture Four, we situated in the interior of Africa. If we state that the Negro race was born of the cooperation between the normal Spirits of Form and the abnormal Spirits of Form centred in Mercury, then from an occult standpoint we are perfectly correct in describing the Negro race as the "Mercury race".

Let us now continue along the line joining the centres or focal points from which the individual races spread outward. We then come to Asia which is the seat of the "Venus race" or the Malayan race. We then move northward across the wide expanse of Asia and we find the Mongolian race which is formed by the Mars forces. Then we cross over into Europe and find the Europeans who in their original racial character are "Jupiter men". If we cross the ocean to America which is the centre where civilizations or races die, we find there dark "Saturn's race", the original Red Indian race. The American Indian race is the "Saturn race". Thus if you look into the matter more closely from an occult standpoint you will become aware of the five centres where the planetary forces are concentrated and are manifested in the external world.

With a progressively more definite and concrete conception of this racial distribution you will develop an inner understanding of the racial characteristics peculiar to the peoples spread over the Earth, an understanding of this unique cooperation of the normal and abnormal Spirits of Form. We have thus sketched the picture as we are able to capture it at a definite moment in time. But what I have said about the different centres on the Earth is again only valid for a specific epoch of evolution. It is valid for the epoch when, at a definite moment of time in the old Atlantean evolution, the peoples began to migrate from a centre in Atlantis and sought the particular centre where they could receive the training appropriate to their race. Hence in my book *Occult Science* I pointed out that in old Atlantis specific Mystery Centres called the Atlantean Oracles were responsible for directing this distribution of peoples over the Earth, so that in effect that state of balance or equilibrium could be achieved which led to the

proper distribution of the races. In one such Mystery Oracle
the truths of which we are now speaking were always investigated
and originally man took his direction entirely from them. In this
manner the events on Earth were determined in accordance with
these spiritual centres.

The wave of peoples who swept across Africa and crystallized
into the Ethiopian race is an expression of an impulse from the
Mercury Oracle in which one could clearly observe the cooperation of the normal Spirits of Form (the six Elohim and Jahve or
Jehovah) and also the participation of the abnormal Spirits of
Form working from the Mercury Centre. The Centre of equilibrium on Earth was selected in accordance with the right astro-
logical conjunction of planetary forces at the various centres
and the point of radiation for the race in question was determined
thereby.

The formation of the other races was determined in a similar
way. In accordance with these determining factors the grand
design is drawn up, charting the cosmic influences in relation
to peoples, families, etc. It is an image of cosmic activity and
reflects the planetary forces which stream down into the Earth,
ray outwards from the Earth and determine man's destiny.

Now how do we look upon a member of the Ethiopian race, of
the Mercury race? We see him as one who was originally chosen,
who was predestined by the Elohim to express the quintessence
of the all-human. But from the Mercury Centre the potent
influences of the abnormal Spirits of Form intervened and modified
the form of man to such an extent that the Ethiopian race arose.
And such was the case with each individual race. The migrations
of the peoples were specifically directed from the original centre;
this is indicated by the line linking the focal points or centres
in my diagram a few days ago. You must therefore imagine the
Spirits of Form radiating from a centre, which, we must assume,
existed at a definite moment of time in old Atlantis. These
Spirits of Form rayed down into the Atlantean continent and
fashioned it in such a way that the human souls were brought
under the dominion of the corresponding abnormal Spirits of
Form.

In this way the broad foundations of the races were laid, and when man looks up into the infinite expanse of the Macrocosm he must seek there the forces out of which he was built up. He is fashioned by their spiritual rays reflected from the Earth-centre. And when he looks up to the normal Spirits of Form, the Elohim, he is looking up to that which actually makes him into man. When he looks up to the forces concentrated in the individual planetary Spirits (with the exception of the Sun and Moon) he perceives the forces which determine his membership of a particular race.

Now how do these Race Spirits work in and upon man? They work in a very unique way; they permeate his vital energies, they penetrate even down into his physical body. Now you know that the four fundamental members of man find their impress and are reflected in corresponding parts of the physical body: the 'I' finds its impress in the blood, the astral body in the nervous system, the etheric or life-body in the glandular system. Only the physical body is self-sufficient; it is a reflection of its own inner being which for the man of the present is subject to its own fixed laws.

Now those spiritual Beings who are stirring in man and determine his racial character cannot at first work directly into his higher vehicles. They are active first of all in these reflections of the higher vehicles in the physical body. They cannot as yet enter directly into the physical body, but they are active in the three other members, in the blood which is the reflection of the 'I'; in the nervous system, the reflection of the astral body; and in the glandular system which is the reflection of the etheric body. The Race Spirits, the abnormal Spirits of Form, are active in these three systems, which are part of man's organic system, but are reflections of the higher vehicles.

Thus the physical body of man is determined from within. These various spiritual Beings invade those members of the physical body which are the preliminary drafts, the suggestions of the higher vehicles. Now where, for instance, does Mercury make his influence felt? Under Mercury, I include all the abnormal Spirits of Form to be found in Mercury. He makes his influence felt by cooperating with others, especially in the glandular system. He is active in the glandular (or lymphatic) system where are manifested the forces born of that preponderance of the Mercury forces which are present in the Ethiopian race. Everything which gives the Ethiopian race its distinctive character stems from the ferment of the Mercury forces in the glandular system of this people. What transforms the undifferentiated universal human from into the distinctive Ethiopian type with his black pigmentation and woolly or frizzy hair is the consequence of their activity.

If you now move over to Asia you will find there likewise the planetary forces of Venus, an abnormal development of the Spirits of Form. By transferring their point of attack principally to what we call the impress of the astral body, these Venus forces work in the nervous system. They work upon the nervous system however in a peculiar way, not directly as Venus spirits. For the nervous system can be worked upon indirectly in two ways. One way is through the respiration. By working especially upon the respiration, these activities of the Venus Spirits are localized in the respiratory and nervous system and give it a definite form. In this indirect way the abnormal Spirits of Form whom we may call Venus Beings work through the respiratory and nervous system in the Malayan race, in the yellowish-brown races found in Southern Asia and in the direction of the Malay Archipelago. Just as the glandular type is found distributed over Ethiopia, so in these regions is found the type of man in whom the abnormal Spirits of Form work upon the nervous system indirectly through the respiratory system. In the nervous system is prepared that which, with special modifications, produces the more or less yellow skinned racial types. The transformation wrought in these races manifests itself more in that part of the nervous system covered by the term 'solar plexus'—not in the higher or central nervous system therefore, but in that mysterious part of the nervous system which runs in two cords parallel with the spinal medulla and branches out in various directions to form a network. This part of the nervous system therefore which from our point of view is not yet associated with higher mental activity, is worked upon indirectly through the respiratory system. The unconscious organism is deeply stirred by these Venus forces which work in these racial types.

Let us now move northward to the wide Mongolian plains where are largely concentrated those Spirits of Form who work indirectly through the forces of the blood. In this geographical area is prepared in the forces of the blood that which brings about a modification of the human species and determines the basic character of the race. There is however a very peculiar feature attaching to the Mongolian race; the Mars Spirits enter into the blood. But they work in the blood in a specific manner. They are able to counteract the influence of the six Elohim who are centred in the Sun. In the Mongolian race, therefore, they work in opposition to these six Elohim. At the same time they actively oppose the influence of Jahve or Jehovah who has withdrawn His field of action from that of the six Elohim. But apart from this interaction of the Mars Spirits with the six Elohim and Jahve which produces the Mongolian race there is another factor of paramount importance which must be taken into consideration. Just as in the one case, the Mars Spirits in opposition to the six Elohim from the Sun and Jahve from the Moon create the Mongolian race, so in another case, we must assume that the Jahve forces from the Moon sphere meet and cooperate with the Mars Spirits and thus a special kind of modification arises, namely, the Semitic race. Here is the occult explanation for the origin of the Semites. The Semitic people are an example of a modification of collective humanity. Jahve or Jehovah shuts Himself off from the other Elohim and invests this people with a special character by cooperating with the Mars Spirits, in order to bring about a special modification of his people. You will now understand the peculiar character of the Semitic people and its mission. In a profound occult sense the Biblical writer was able to claim that Jahve or Jehovah had made this people his own. If you add to this the fact that Jahve cooperated with the Mars Spirits who worked principally in the blood, you will understand why racial continuity through the blood-stream was of particular importance to the Semitic-Hebrew people and why Jahve describes Himself as the God who is present in the blood of the generations, in the blood of Abraham, Isaac and Jacob. When he declared himself to be the God of Abraham, Isaac and Jacob, He proclaimed that He was present in the blood-stream of the

Patriarchs. Whatsoever works in the blood, whatsoever must be determined through the blood—the cooperation with the Mars Spirits—that is one of the mysteries which give us a deep insight into the wise guidance of all mankind.

The blood of mankind is thus subject to a twofold influence; two races emerge, the Mongolian race and the Semitic race. This points to the existence of an important polarity in mankind and we must emphasize the immense importance of this polarity if we wish to plumb the depths of the Folk Souls.

We must now turn our attention to the Western centre and trace the way in which dynamic forces of the Spirits and Beings who are centred in Jupiter operate in man. These elect to work directly upon the nervous system via the outer life of the senses. This is the one way. In the other, the planetary forces work into the sympathetic nervous system, entering indirectly into the solar plexus through the respiratory system. Now the Jupiter forces work indirectly through the sense-impressions and from there radiate to those parts of the central nervous system which are situated in the brain and spinal cord. Here is the seat of those forces which determine the particular racial character of those races belonging to the Jupiter humanity. This applies more or less to the Aryans, to the peoples of Asia Minor and Europe whom we regard as members of the Caucasian race. In these peoples the modification of the generic character which stems from the abnormal Spirits of Form is accounted for by the influence upon the senses of the abnormal Spirits whom we may describe as Jupiter Spirits. The Caucasians therefore are determined through the senses.

Now you will also understand why a people like the Greeks who were consciously under the special influence of Jupiter or Zeus and who felt themselves to be a focal point for the Zeus influence, were predominantly determined by what flows into the nervous system via the senses. The Greeks, of course, were also influenced by the forces of the Elohim which stream in from the Sun. But the Greeks dedicated everything that acts upon the senses to the service of Jupiter or Zeus and so achieved greatness. To them all external forms, all forms of external life were imbued with deeper meaning. They perceived the spiritual in the physical

and hence became the chief exponents of sculpture and archi-
tectonic forms. We have here indicated the very special mission
of the Greek people who are so preeminently the people of Jupiter
or Zeus. Even at the time when, especially under the influence
of the new planetary constellation, the cooperation of the Jupiter
or Zeus forces with the universal Elohim forces took place, they
felt themselves to be the people of Zeus.

All the peoples of South-West Asia, and especially the European peoples are, on the whole, modifications of this Jupiter
influence and you can well imagine that as man has many senses,
many modifications are possible and that in the formation of the
individual peoples within this root race, peoples who were
formed by the influence of the senses upon the nervous system,
one or other of the senses may predominate. Consequently the
various peoples may assume the most diverse forms. According
as the eye or the ear or one of the other senses predominates,
so will the different peoples respond in this or that way to the
particular national tendency within the racial character. In
consequence of this they are faced with quite specific tasks.
The particular task of the Caucasian race is to find the way
to the spirit through the senses, for this race is orientated chiefly
towards the sense-world.

Here is disclosed something that introduces us to the deeper
secrets of occultism; it shows how, in those peoples who are
subject to the Venus forces, the initial steps in development,
even in occult development, must be concentrated on the respiratory system. Amongst the peoples living more in the Western
Hemisphere, on the other hand, the initial steps must start from
an enrichment and a spiritualization of the life of the senses.
This is experienced by those peoples inhabiting countries more
towards the West in their stages of higher cognition, in Imagination, Inspiration and Intuition, in so far as the Jupiter Spirit
originally modified the character.

Hence these two geographical centres were always present in
human evolution, the one presided over by the Spirits of Venus,
the other by those of Jupiter. The Jupiter Spirits in particular
were perceived in those Mysteries in which—as those of you will

know who attended my lecture-course in Munich last year*—the three Individualities ultimately came together, the three spiritual Beings, Buddha, Zarathustra or Zarathas in his later incarnation, and that great leader of humanity, Skythianos. This is the "Council" or spiritual conference which, under the guidance of One still greater, set itself the task of investigating the mysterious forces which must be developed for the evolution of humanity, forces which originated from that centre initially connected with the Jupiter forces and which was pre-ordained in the chart of the cultural centres already mentioned.

Finally, the abnormal Spirits of Form who have their centre in Saturn work indirectly via all the other systems into the glandular system. In the Saturn race, therefore, in everything to which we must ascribe the Saturn character, we must expect to find the combination of the forces leading to the twilight of mankind, forces which set the seal upon its development and sow the seeds of its ultimate decline. This action and its effect upon the glandular system can be seen in the American Indian race and was the cause of its ultimate extinction. The Saturn influence finally works via all the other systems into the glandular system which secretes the hardest parts of man. This slow decline is characterized by a kind of ossification which is clearly reflected in the external form. If you look at the pictures of the old American Indians the process of ossification described above is evident in the decline of this race. In a race such as this everything pertaining to the forces of the Saturn evolution has become realized in a special manner; then Saturn withdrew into itself, abandoned man to his bony system and thus hastened his decline. One feels something of this truly occult activity if one observes how, in the nineteenth century, a representative of these old American Indians still preserves a memory of that great Atlantean civilization which could not adapt itself to later evolution. There exists a description of a beautiful scene in which a chieftain of this moribund Red Indian race confronts a European colonist. Imagine the conflicting emotions when two such men confront each other, the one representing those who came from Europe,

* *The East in the Light of the West. The Children of Lucifer and the Brothers of Christ.* Nine lectures given in Munich, 23rd–29th August, 1909.

and the other those who, in the earliest ages, at the time of the separation of the races, moved Westward. The Red Indian brought over to the West all that was great in the Atlantean culture. What the Red Indian valued most highly was that he was still able dimly to sense something of the former greatness and majesty of a period which existed in the old Atlantean epoch when the separation of the races had hardly begun, when man could look up to the Sun and perceive the Spirits of Form through a sea of mist. Through an ocean of mist the Atlantean was clairvoyantly aware of the seven Spirits of Form acting in concert. And this cooperative activity was called by the Atlanteans the Great Spirit who revealed himself to man in ancient Atlantis. The Atlantean had not assimilated all that the Venus, Mercury, Mars and Jupiter Spirits brought about in the East, to whom we owe all the civilizations which reached their zenith in Europe in the middle of the nineteenth century. The descendant of the brown race did not participate in this development. He held firm to the Great Spirit of the primeval past. He became aware of achievements of the Europeans (who, in a remote past, had also known the Great Spirit) when a piece of paper was laid before him on which were many little symbols, letters, of which he understood nothing. All that was alien to him, for in his soul still dwelt the Great Spirit. The speech he made has been preserved to us and it is noteworthy because it provides evidence of what we have already indicated. It runs somewhat as follows: "Here in the soil, trampled beneath the feet of the conquerors the bones of my brothers lie buried. Why are the feet of our conquerors allowed to desecrate the graves of my brothers? Because they are in possession of that which makes the White Man great. But there is something else which makes the Brown Man great; it is the Great Spirit who speaks to him in the soughing of the wind, in the murmuring of the forest, in the surging of the waves, in the purling of the brook, in thunder and in lightning! That is the Spirit who to us speaks truth. Yes, from the lips of the Great Spirit comes truth. But your spirits here on paper and who express what to you is great, they do not speak the truth." Thus spoke the Indian chieftain from his point of view. "Redskin is servant of the Great Spirit; Paleface is servant of the spirits who, in black shapes resembling pygmy beings"—he was referring to the letters—"dance on the paper; they do not speak the truth". This dialogue of historic importance was exchanged between the conqueror and the last of the great chieftains of the Red Indians. Here we have an example of the Saturn forces and their activity and of what follows from the cooperation between Saturn and other Spirits at such a moment as this when two contrasting civilizations meet.

Thus we have seen how here on Earth the birth of universal humanity was prepared by the Elohim or the normal Spirits of Form, how then the five principal races of human evolution detach themselves from the collective body of mankind, from the teaming mass of humanity, and how these five races are related to the guiding Spirits in the Hierarchy of the abnormal Spirits of Form, races whom we must name after the five planets, whereas the normal Spirits of Form are centred in the Sun and in the Moon. From here we shall pass on to something which will be easier to understand, because we shall be able to relate it to something familiar to us, namely, to tribes and peoples.

LECTURE SEVEN

Advance of Folk Spirits to the Rank of Time Spirits.
Monotheism and Pluralism. Exoteric and Esoteric Christianity.

If you enter into the spirit of the lectures given here in the last
few days you will be able to accept the idea that not only do the
Beings and forces of the various Hierarchies guide and direct
events upon our Earth and especially the course of human
evolution, but also that the Beings of these Hierarchies themselves undergo evolution or development. We spoke of how the
Beings of a particular Hierarchy intervene in order to direct the
evolution of a particular race, how, for example, as normal and
abnormal Spirits of Form they cooperate to organize the various
races.

Now the question which confronts us is whether these spiritual
Beings themselves advance to a higher rank. When we look back
over the post-Atlantean times we are conscious that in the
course of their development certain spiritual Beings advance to
the next higher rank. Since the Atlantean catastrophe, since the
beginning of the post-Atlantean evolution, we are living in an
Age when certain Archangels, certain Beings of the Hierarchy
of the Archangeloi, advance to the rank of the Archai or Time
Spirits. This is a most interesting phenomenon, for when we
observe how the Folk Spirits, or Archangels in our terminology,
rise to a higher rank, only then do we have a true understanding
of cosmic events. This advance in rank is connected with the
fact that in late Atlantis and for some time after, the distribution
of mankind, the distribution of races, has been followed by a
second migration of peoples. If we wish to understand the period
when the division of mankind into the five root races of which we
have already spoken took place, we must look far back into early
Atlantean times. If we wish to ascertain when those who became

the black or Ethiopian race migrated to a particular geographical area in Africa, when those who became the Malayan race migrated to Southern Asia, then we must look back to early Atlantean times. Later on, other migrations followed upon these early migrations.

Whilst, therefore, the Earth was already colonized by the nuclei of these peoples, other peoples were despatched to those geographical areas of the Earth already colonized. Thus we meet with a second migration in later Atlantean times. If we wish to understand the pattern and extent of the distribution of races in Europe, Africa, and America at the time of the gradual submergence of Atlantis, and the later great migration towards the end of the Atlantean epoch, when a small band first set out during the post-Atlantean epoch, then we must clearly realize that we are here dealing with that mighty stream of humanity which pushed forward into Asia, into Indian territory, and that, as has often been pointed out, the nuclei of future peoples remained behind at different points and from these nuclei were developed the various peoples of Asia, Africa and Europe. We are here concerned therefore with an earlier distribution and a later expansion, with a second wave. The purpose of this second wave was to despatch in a West-East direction those folk communities who were each under the guidance of an Archangel. But these Archangels who were the spiritual Powers directing these tribes or folk communities were at different stages of development; in other words, some were nearer than others to the rank of a Time Spirit or Spirit of the Age. We have to look to the Far East for that movement of peoples whose Archangel was the first to attain the rank of a Time Spirit. This was the stream which merged with the original inhabitants of India and formed the ruling class of that country and so laid the foundations of the first post-Atlantean civilization after their Archangel had been promoted to be the first Time Spirit or Archai-being of the post-Atlantean civilization. Now this Time Spirit directed the sacred culture of ancient India and made it the leading culture of the first post-Atlantean epoch. Meanwhile the other peoples of Asia who were gradually developing, were for a long time simply under the direction of Archangels.

The peoples of Europe also who had remained behind during the migration from West to East had long been under the guidance of Archangels when the Archangel of India had already risen to the rank of an Archai-being who then worked through intuition upon those great teachers of India, the Holy Rishis. Through the mediation of this exalted and important Spirit the Rishis were able to fulfil their high mission in the manner already described. This Time Spirit worked on for a long time, whilst the people lying to the North of ancient India were still under the guidance of the Archangel. After the Time Spirit of India had fulfilled his mission he was promoted to lead the entire evolution of post-Atlantean humanity.

In the Old Persian epoch the Archangel became the Spirit of Personality, the Time Spirit, from whom the great Zarathustra or Zoroaster, the original Zarathustra, received his inspiration. This again is an example of an Archangel, a Folk Soul who has risen to the rank of Time Spirit. As we stated at the beginning of this lecture, we are experiencing the same situation today, namely, that the Archangels, in the course of fulfilling their mission, advance to the rank of guiding and ruling Spirits of the Age.

In the Egypto-Chaldean epoch, the Archangel of the Egyptian people and the Archangel of the Chaldean people, both rose to a higher rank. During this epoch the Archangel of the Egyptian people rose to the rank of a leading Time Spirit and took over the guidance and control of that which formerly devolved upon the Chaldean Archangel. The leader in the Egypto-Chaldean age thus became the third mighty, guiding Time Spirit who had gradually advanced beyond the rank of the Egyptian Archangel. But this was also the epoch in which another important development took place, a development which ran parallel with the Egypto-Chaldean civilization and is related to the development to which we drew special attention in our last lecture.

We have seen that everything associated with the Semitic tribes assumed a special significance, and that from amongst the Semitic race Jahve or Jehovah had chosen a Semitic people to be his chosen people. Since he had chosen a particular race to be his special people, He needed at first, whilst this race was gradually developing, a kind of Archangel to act as his vice-regent. In ancient times, therefore, the evolving Semitic people was guided by an Archangel who was under the continuous inspiration of Jahve or Jehovah and afterwards this Archangel himself grew to be a Time Spirit. Apart from the ordinary evolving Time Spirits of the Old Indian, Old Persian and Old Chaldean peoples therefore, there was yet another Time Spirit who played his own special part by working within a particular people. This is a Time Spirit who, in a certain respect, appears in the mission of a Nation Spirit, a Time Spirit whom we must call the Semitic Nation Spirit. His task was of a very special kind. You will understand this if you bear in mind that, in reality, this particular people was singled out from the normal course of evolution for special guidance. Through these special arrangements this people was entrusted with a mission which was of particular importance for the post-Atlantean epoch and which was distinguished from the missions of all other peoples. One can best understand this mission of the Semitic people by comparing it with the missions of the various peoples of the post-Atlantean epoch.

Mankind is subject to two spiritual currents. The one has its starting-point in monadology or pluralism* to give it its correct name. This theory recognizes more than one ultimate principle in ontology. Wherever you turn you will find that in some form or other the peoples of the post-Atlantean epoch started from a plurality of aspects of the Divine—the trinity of ancient India, later symbolized in the figures of Brahma, Shiva and Vishnu; the trinity of Odin, Hönir and Lödur of German mythology. You will find a trinity everywhere and this trinity subdivided into a plurality. This characteristic is peculiar not only to myths and teachings about the Gods, but also to philosophies where we meet it again in the form of monadology. This is the one current which, because it starts from pluralism or monadology can offer the greatest possible variety. It was in the post-Atlantean epoch

*Note by translator—*Pluralism:* the theory which recognizes more than one ultimate principle in ontology. *Monadology:* doctrine of monads as formulated by Leibnitz. *Monism:* the doctrine that attempts to explain the phenomena of the Cosmos by one ultimate substance.

that, starting from the farthest East in India and following a wide curve through Asia to Europe, this doctrine of pluralism which after all is expressed in Anthroposophy by our recognition of a number of widely differing Beings and Hierarchies, has been represented in the most diverse ways and in a wide variety of forms.

The polarity to pluralism was monism, the doctrine that one principle of being or ultimate substance constitutes the underlying reality of the physical world. The real inspirers of the worship of a single divinity, those who gave the impulse towards monotheism and monism are the Semitic peoples. It is natural to them, and if you recall what I said in this morning's lecture, it is their mission to represent the one God, the Monon.

He who, surveying the Universe, persisted in explaining the phenomena of the Cosmos by a single ultimate principle, a monon, would remain prisoner of his limitations. Monism or monotheism in itself can only represent an ultimate ideal; it could never lead to a real understanding of the world, to a comprehensive, concrete view of the world. Nevertheless, in the post-Atlantean age the current of monotheism also had to be represented, so that the urge, the impulse towards monotheism devolved upon a single people, the Semitic people. The monistic principle is reflected in this people by a certain rigidity or inflexibility, whilst all the other peoples, in so far as their different divinities are comprehended in a unity, receive the impulse towards monism from them. The monistic impulse has always come from the Semitic people. The other peoples are inclined to pluralism.

It is extremely important that this should be borne in mind and whoever is concerned with the continuance of the old Hebraic impulse will find the extremes of monotheism at the present day amongst the learned Rabbis, in Rabbinism. The task of this particular people is to propagate the doctrine that a single ultimate principle underlies the world. The task of all other nations, peoples and Time Spirits was analytic, to represent the one World-Principle as articulated into different Beings. In India, for example, the ultimate abstraction of the Unity underlying all things was divided into a tri-unity, just as the one

God of Christianity is divided into Three Persons. The task of the other nations was to 'analyse' ultimate Reality and so to furnish particular aspects of it with plentiful content, to fill themselves with rich material for those representations which can apprehend phenomena with sympathetic understanding. The task of the Semitic people was to eschew all pluralism and to devote itself to synthesis, to the doctrine of one substance. Hence the power of speculation, the power of synthetic thought which is illustrated by Cabbalism is unsurpassed precisely because it stems from this impulse.

Everything that could possibly be distilled from the unitary principle by the synthesizing activity of the 'I' has been distilled by the Semitic spirit in the course of thousands of years. This is the significance of the Semitic influence in the world and illustrates the polarity between pluralism and monism. Monism is not possible without pluralism. Pluralism is not possible without monism. We must recognize the necessity for both.

The language of objective fact often leads to quite different conclusions from those which are motivated by the prevailing sympathies or antipathies. Therefore we must have a clear understanding of the tasks of the individual Folk Spirits. Whereas the leaders of the several peoples in Asia and Africa had long since risen to the rank of Time Spirits or Spirits of Personality and indeed some of them were expecting to transform themselves from Time Spirits to the next higher rank, to Spirits of Form— just as, for example, that Time Spirit who was active in ancient India had already risen in certain respects to the rank of the Spirits of Form—the several peoples of Europe were for a long time still under the direction of their individual Archangels. It was not until the fourth post-Atlantean epoch that the Archangel of ancient Greece rose above the various peoples of Europe who were still under the guidance of their Archangels to the rank of a Time Spirit. He became the leading Time Spirit of the fourth post-Atlantean epoch, the Graeco-Latin epoch. Thus the Archangel of Greece advanced to the rank of an Archai-being, a Spirit of Personality. After he had become a Time Spirit, the influence of this Greek Archangel extended far and wide through Asia, Africa and Europe who looked to Hellas for their culture.

Whilst the Archangel of the Greeks had developed into an Archai-being, the Time Spirit of the Egyptians and of the Persians had advanced in evolution towards the Hierarchy of the Spirits of Form. We are now about to touch upon something exceptionally interesting in the course of post-Atlantean evolution. As a consequence of his earlier development the Greek Archangel was able to pass relatively quickly through that stage of development which qualified him for a specially prominent position as Spirit of the Age (Time Spirit). Something therefore of the greatest significance occurred in the fourth post-Atlantean epoch.

Now at that time there took place, as we know, the Mystery of Golgotha through which mankind received the Christ Impulse. This Impulse was destined in the course of the following centuries and millennia to spread gradually over the whole Earth. Without this consummation of Golgotha, without the activity of certain guiding and directing Beings from the ranks of the Hierarchies, this could not have been achieved. A most remarkable and interesting event now occurred. At a definite moment of time which coincided approximately with the descent of Christ upon Earth, the Greek Time Spirit renounced for our present epoch the possibility of rising into the Hierarchy of the Spirits of Form and became the guiding Time Spirit who then works on through the successive epochs. He became the representative guiding Spirit of exoteric Christianity, so that the Archai-being himself, the guiding Spirit of the Greeks, himself formed the vanguard of the Christ Impulse. In consequence, ancient Greece rapidly declined at the time of the expansion of Christianity because it had surrendered its guiding Time Spirit in order that he might become the leader of exoteric Christianity. The Greek Time Spirit then became the missionary, the inspirer or rather the intuiting Spirit of the expanding exoteric Christianity. Here we have a concrete example of an act of renunciation such as we have spoken of. Because the Greek Time Spirit had fulfilled his mission in the fourth post-Atlantean age so admirably, he could now advance in evolution towards a higher Hierarchy. But he renounced this possibility and by so doing became the guiding

Spirit of the expanding exoteric Christianity, and in that capacity he continued to work among the various peoples.

A similar act of renunciation took place on another occasion, and this second instance is of particular interest to students of Spiritual Science. Whilst in Asia, including Egypt and Greece, the several Archangels were advancing to the rank of Time Spirits, there existed in Europe isolated peoples and tribes who were guided by their several Archangels. Thus, whilst the corresponding Archangels who had been sent in ancient times from the West towards the East had advanced to the rank of Time Spirits, there still existed in Europe an Archangel who worked in the Germanic and especially in the Celtic peoples, in those peoples who, at the time of the founding of Christianity, were still spread over a large area of Western Europe extending into Hungary, Southern Germany and the Alpine countries. These peoples had the Celtic Folk Spirit as their Archangel. The peoples belonging to the Celtic Folk Spirit also inhabited an area extending far into the North East of Europe. They were guided by an important Archangel who, soon after the Christian impulse had been bestowed on mankind, had renounced the possibility of becoming an Archai-being, a Spirit of Personality, and elected to remain at the Archangel stage and to subordinate himself in future to the different Time Spirits who might arise in Europe. Hence the Celtic peoples also declined as a united people because their Archangel had made a special act of renunciation and had undertaken a special mission. This is a typical example of how, in such a case, an act of renunciation helps to initiate particular missions.

Now what became of the Archangel of the Celtic peoples after he had renounced the possibility of becoming a Spirit of Person-ality? He became the inspirer of esoteric Christianity. All the underlying teachings and impulses of esoteric Christianity, especially of the real, true esoteric Christianity, have their source in his inspirations. The hidden sanctuary for those who were initiated into these Mysteries was situated in Western Europe and there the spiritual impulse was imparted by this guiding Spirit who had originally undergone an important training as Archangel of the Celtic people, had renounced his promotion to

a higher rank and had undertaken another mission—that of
becoming the inspirer of esoteric Christianity which was destined
to live on further in the Mysteries of the Holy Grail, in Rosicrucianism. Here is an example of an act of renunciation, a
sacrifice on the part of one of these Beings of the Hierarchies. At
the same time it offers a concrete example illustrating the significance of this sacrifice. Although this Archangel could have
advanced to the rank of an Archai-being, he remained at the
Archangel stage and in consequence was able to guide the
important current of esoteric Christianity whose influence is
destined to be furthered through the medium of the different
Time Spirits. No matter how these Time Spirits may work, this
esoteric Christianity will remain a living source, able to be
renewed and metamorphosed ever and again under the influence
of different epochs. Here then is another example illustrating an
act of renunciation, whilst we, on the other hand, are witnessing
in our age especially the mighty spectacle of Folk Spirits advancing to the rank of Time Spirits.

Now the various Germanic peoples of Europe had originally
been guided by a single Archangel-being and were destined to
come gradually under the guidance of many different Archangels in order to become differentiated. It is of course extremely
difficult to speak impartially of these things without arousing
jealousy and emotional prejudice. Consequently certain mysteries
pertaining to this evolution can only be touched upon lightly.
From among these Archangels emerged the Archai-being, the
leading Time Spirit of our fifth post-Atlantean epoch, long after
one of the Archangels of the Germanic peoples had undergone a
certain preparatory training. The Time Spirit who was the
Folk Spirit in the Graeco-Latin age became, as you know, that
Time Spirit who was later concerned in the expansion of exoteric
Christianity. Later Roman history was also guided by a kind of
Time Spirit who had risen from the rank of Archangel of the
ancient Romans and had joined forces with the Christian Time
Spirit in order to coordinate their activities. Both of these were
the teachers of that Archangel who guided the Germanic peoples,
had been one of their guiding Archangels and had then risen to
the rank of the Time Spirit of the fifth post-Atlantean epoch. But

much still remained to be done. It was essential that the different folk elements in the peoples of Europe should be mingled and individualized. This was only possible for the following reasons: —whereas, in Asia and Africa the Archangels had long since advanced to the rank of Time Spirits, Europe was still under the guidance of the Archangels themselves. The individual peoples, indifferent to the Time Spirits and guided by their several Folk Souls, were wholly given up to the impulses of the Folk Spirit. At the time when the Christian impulse began to pervade mankind, Europe was the scene of the simultaneous activity of many Folk Spirits, filled with a spirit of liberty, each acting independently and who therefore made it difficult for a Time Spirit of the fifth epoch to arise who could direct the several Folk Spirits. The French people, for example, was the product of the intermixture of Celts, Franks and Latins, and in consequence the entire guidance naturally followed a clearly defined pattern. It passed from the several guiding Archangels, who had been given other tasks, into the hands of others. We have already indicated what was the mission of the guiding Archangel of the Celts; in the same way we could indicate what were the missions of the Archangels of the other peoples. Hence amongst the peoples who were products of miscegenation, other Archangels appeared who took over when the various elements intermingled. Thus, over a long period of time—and even in the Middle Ages—the leadership in Central and Northern Europe was chiefly in the hands of the Archangels who were only gradually influenced by that common Time Spirit who was in the vanguard of the Christ Impulse. The several Folk Spirits in Europe frequently became the servants of the Christian Time Spirit. The European Archangels placed themselves in the service of this universal Christian Time Spirit whilst the several peoples were hardly in a position to permit any of the Archangels to advance to the rank of a Time Spirit. Starting from the twelfth century, it was not until the sixteenth and seventeenth centuries that the first steps were undertaken towards the development of the guiding Time Spirit of the fifth post-Atlantean epoch who still directs us today. He belongs to the great leading Time Spirits, equally with those who were the great directing Time Spirits during the Egypto-

Chaldean-Babylonian, Old Persian and Indian epochs. But this Spirit of our fifth post-Atlantean epoch worked in a very unique manner. He had, in effect, to enter into a kind of compromise with one of the former Time Spirits who were active before the birth of the Christian impulse, namely, with the Time Spirit of ancient Egypt, who as we have heard, had risen in a certain respect to the rank of a Spirit of Form. Thus, our present fifth post-Atlantean epoch is really governed by a Time Spirit who in a certain way is very much subject to the influence and impulses of the Time Spirit of ancient Egypt and who is a Spirit of Form at an elementary stage.

This was the source of the many cleavages and divisions of our time. In the fifth post-Atlantean epoch our Time Spirit is striving to lift himself to the Spiritual, and to raise the fifth post-Atlantean epoch to a higher stage. But this does not exclude a tendency or inclination to materialism. According as the various Archangels, the various Folk Souls, are more or less inclined towards this materialist tendency, so there emerges under the guidance of this Time Spirit of the fifth post-Atlantean epoch a more or less materialistic people who inclines the Spirit of the Age more in the direction of materialism. On the other hand an idealistic people inclines the Spirit of the Age more towards idealism.

Now from the twelfth to the sixteenth century something gradually developed, working (in a certain respect) parallel with the Christian Time Spirit—who continues the activity of the Greek Time Spirit—so that in fact, in a remarkable manner, there streamed into our culture the Christian Time Spirit united with a Time Spirit proper of the fifth post-Atlantean epoch; and again there was an influx of impulses from ancient Egypt whose Time Spirit had advanced to a certain rank among the Spirits of Form. Now precisely because such a trifolium is at work in our whole culture it has been possible for Folk Souls and cultural patterns of widely differing kinds and complexions to emerge in the fifth post-Atlantean epoch. It became possible for the Time Spirit to manifest the greatest diversity. The Archangels who took their orders from the Time Spirit worked in many different ways.

Those of you who live in Scandinavia will be interested in something which we shall go into closely in our next lectures. The following question will be of particular interest to you: What form did the activity of that Archangel take who was once upon a time sent to Norway with the Nordic peoples, the Scandinavian peoples, and from whom the various Archangels of Europe, especially those of Western, Central and Northern Europe, received their inspirations? In the eyes of the world it would be regarded as the height of folly to speak of that spiritual centre on the continent of Europe which at one time radiated the most powerful spiritual impulses, the centre which was the seat of exalted Spirits before the Celtic Folk Spirit as Celtic Archangel had established a new centre in the High Castle of the Grail. The Archangel of the Northern peoples first received his mission from that place which in ancient times had been the spiritual centre of Europe. It must seem the height of folly, as I said, if we were to indicate as the central source of inspiration for the various Germanic tribes that district which now lies over Central Germany—not actually on the Earth, but hovering above it. If you were to describe an arc to include the towns of Detmold and Paderborn, you would then delimit the region from where the most exalted Spirits were sent on their several missions to Northern and Western Europe. Hence, because the great centre of spiritual inspiration was situated there, legend tells of Asgard having been actually located at this place on Earth. There, in the remote past, was the great centre of inspiration; in later years its spiritual mission was taken over by the Castle of the Grail.

The peoples of Scandinavia, with their first Archangels, were at that time endowed with quite different potentialities, potentialities which at the present time are reflected only in the peculiar configuration of Scandinavian mythology. If we compare in the occult sense, Scandinavian mythology with other mythologies, we may know that this Norse mythology depicts the native predisposition of the Archangel who was sent upon his mission to Scandinavia, that native predisposition which has retained its original form and which is peculiar to a child whose particular talents, latent gifts, etc., remain at a childlike stage. The Archangel who was sent to Scandinavia embodies those potentialities which were later expressed in the peculiar configuration of Scandinavian mythology. Here lies the signal importance of Scandinavian mythology for the understanding of the real, inner being of the Scandinavian Folk Soul. Herein, too, lies the great significance which the understanding of this mythology has for the further development of this Archangel who certainly has the potentiality to rise to the rank of an Archai-being. But to this end he must develop in a specific way those native potentialities which (in certain respects) have been overshadowed by the rising influence of that Time Spirit who was in the vanguard of exoteric Christianity. Although Germanic-Scandinavian mythology and Greek mythology are in many respects curiously alike, I must point out nevertheless that there is no other mythology which, in its peculiar composition and characteristic development, gives a deeper or clearer picture of cosmic evolution than does this Scandinavian mythology, so that this picture may serve as a preliminary sketch for the anthroposophical view of world-evolution.

Thus Germanic mythology, from the way in which it was developed out of the native powers of the Archangel, is in its pictures closely akin to the anthroposophical conception of the world such as it shall grow to be in the course of time for all mankind. The problem will be how those original, native potentialities of an Archangel can be developed after he has been nurtured by the Christian Time Spirit. These potentialities will be able to become an important element in the guiding Time Spirit when, at a later stage in the evolution of a people, this people has learned how to develop and perfect the potentialities with which it was endowed at an earlier epoch. In this connection we have only indicated an important problem, an important evolution of an European Archangel. We have indicated to what extent he has the potentiality to develop into a Time Spirit. We shall stop at this point for the moment. We shall then continue our investigations, when we shall endeavour, by analysing the configuration of the Folk Soul, to undertake an esoteric study of mythology, and a special section will be devoted to a description of the very interesting characteristics of Germanic mythology, and also of Scandinavian mythology in particular.

LECTURE EIGHT

The five post-Atlantean Civilizations. Greek and Teutonic Mythology.

If we wish to study the development of Germanic-Nordic history and the spiritual impulses embodied therein, we must first of all bear in mind the fundamental character of Teutonic mythology. In the last lecture I pointed out that this Teutonic mythology, despite its many points of similarity with other mythologies, is nevertheless something quite unique. It is true, however, that among the Germanic peoples and tribes of Europe there was a large measure of agreement on fundamental conceptions of mythology so that in the regions far to the South it was possible for a uniform view of mythology to exist and, on the whole, a similar understanding of the kindred relationships between those mythologies. At one time there must have been identical understanding of the unique character of the Teutonic mythology throughout all the countries where this mythology, in one form or another, existed. The common features of Teutonic mythology are very different from the essential characteristic of Greek mythology, to say nothing of the Egyptian. Everything in Teutonic mythology is interrelated and differs widely from the substance of Graeco-Roman mythology. At the present time it is not easy to understand this essential element because—on account of certain intellectual assumptions which are outside the scope of the present lecture—there is a general tendency today to embark on the study of comparative religion. But this is a field in which it is possible to perpetuate the greatest nonsense. What happens as a rule when a person compares the mythologies and religions of various peoples with one another? He compares the superficial aspects of the stories of the gods and attempts to demonstrate that the figure of a particular god which appears in one mythology is also found in a like manner in another mythology, and so on. To anyone who knows the real facts this comparative study of religions shows a most disquieting trend in the anthropological studies of the present day, because it is everywhere the practice to compare externals. The impression created by the comparative studies of religions upon one who knows the facts is comparable to the impression made by someone who declares: "Thirty years ago I made the acquaintance of a man; he wore a uniform consisting of blue trousers, red coat, and some kind of head-gear, and so on." Then he rapidly adds: "Twenty years ago I became acquainted with a man who wore the same uniform and ten years ago I met another who also wore the same uniform." Now if the person in question were to believe that, because the men with whom he became acquainted thirty, twenty and ten years ago wore the same uniform, they could therefore be compared with one another in respect of their essential being, he could be greatly mistaken, for a totally different person might be wearing that uniform at those different times. The essential thing is to know what sort of man is concealed behind the uniform. This parallel may seem farfetched, yet in comparative religion it is tantamount to comparing Adonis to Christ. One is merely comparing externals. The apparel and the characteristics of the Beings in the various legends may be very similar or even alike, but the point is to know what is the nature of the divine-spiritual Beings concealed behind them. If completely different Beings are present in Adonis and in Christ, then we are merely comparing externals and the parallel has only superficial value. Nevertheless this comparative method is extremely popular at the present day. Therefore the results of the extensive research in the comparative study of religion with its purely external approach are not of the least consequence. The point is, rather, that one should learn to know to some extent from an understanding of the specific differences of the Folk Spirits the manner in which a particular people arrived at its mythology or other teachings about the gods, or even at its philosophy.

We can scarcely understand the fundamental character of Teutonic mythology unless we review once more the five successive ages of civilization in the post-Atlantean epoch. These five ages of civilization were brought about by migrations from West to East, so that at the end of these migrations the most mature, the most advanced human beings pushed forward into Indian territory and founded there the sacred primeval Indian civilization. The next civilization, and nearer to our own age, was the Persian which was followed by the Egypto-Chaldean-Babylonian, then the Graeco-Latin civilization and finally by our own.

The essential nature of these five civilizations can only be understood if one realizes that in past ages those who participated in them, including also the Angels, the Folk Spirits or Archangels and Time Spirits, were all quite different from one another. Today we propose to devote more attention to the way in which the human beings who participated in these civilizations differed from one another.

The men who, in ancient India for example, founded the ancient Indian civilization—which then found its literary expression in the Vedas and later Indian literature—were totally different from the Graeco-Latin peoples. They were different from the Persian, from the Egypto-Chaldean peoples and most of all from those peoples who were being prepared in Europe for the fifth post-Atlantean civilization. In what respect did they differ? The entire make-up of the members of the ancient Indian peoples was completely different from that of the inhabitants of all the countries lying further West. The peoples of ancient India had reached a high stage of evolution before they developed the 'I'. In all other aspects of evolution they had made great strides. Behind them lay a very long period of development, but they had lived through it in a kind of dim consciousness. Then the 'I' entered in—they awoke to consciousness of the 'I'. Amongst the Indians this came comparatively late, at a time when the people was already to a certain extent very mature, when they had already undergone what the Teutonic peoples still had to undergo when they had developed their ego. Bear this carefully in mind. The Teutonic peoples had to experience with their fully developed 'I' what the inhabitants of ancient India had passed through in a dim state of consciousness, without a developed ego-consciousness.

Now what was the nature of the development which humanity

could undergo in the post-Atlantean epoch? In the old Atlantean times human beings were still endowed with a high degree of the old dim clairvoyance with which they saw into the divine-spiritual world. They had an insight into the hidden workings of that world. Now imagine yourselves for a moment in old Atlantis before the migrations towards the East had begun. The air was still permeated with water-vapour and misty exhalations. The soul of man was different too. He could not yet differentiate between the various external sense-perceptions; at that time he found the spiritual content of the world seemingly diffused around him like a spiritual aura. Thus he possessed a certain natural clairvoyance which he had to overcome. This was achieved by the operation of the forces to whose influence human beings were subject when migrating from West to East. In the course of these migrations man underwent many different stages of spiritual development. There were peoples who, during their migration eastward, at first slept through, as it were, the period of emergence from the old clairvoyance and had already reached a higher stage of development when their ego was still in a dim state of consciousness. They went through various stages of development, but their 'I' was still in a dull, dreamlike condition. The Indians were the furthest evolved when their ego awoke to full self-consciousness. They were so far advanced that they possessed a rich inner soul-life which no longer showed any traces of that elementary stage in soul development which still persisted for a long period of time in the peoples of Europe. The Indians had already undergone that elementary stage a long time before. They awoke to self-consciousness when they were already endowed with spiritual powers and spiritual capacities which enabled them to penetrate deeply into the spiritual worlds. Hence all the activity and positive influence of the various Angels and Archangels on the human souls had become a matter of complete indifference to the more advanced members of the Indian people in their efforts to emerge from their old twilight conditions of clairvoyance. They had no direct consciousness of the work of the Archangels and Angels and all those spiritual Beings who were active, particularly in the folk-spirit. All the work of these higher Beings upon their souls, upon their astral and etheric bodies, was accomplished at a time when they were not yet ego-conscious. They awoke to ego-consciousness when their souls had already reached a very high stage of development. The most advanced among them were able, after a brief development, to read again in the Akashic Record all that had formerly taken place in the evolution of humanity, so that they gazed out into their spiritual environment, into the Cosmos, and could read in the Akashic Record what was taking place in the spiritual world and what they had undergone in a dim twilight state of consciousness. They were unconsciously guided into higher spheres. Before their ego-consciousness had awakened they had acquired spiritual capacities that were much richer than those of the Western peoples. Thus the spiritual world could be directly observed by these men. The most advanced among those who guided the Indian people had risen to such high spiritual levels that, at the time when their ego awoke, they were no longer dependent upon the ego in order to observe how human development sprang forth, so to speak, from the Spirits of Form or Powers, but were more intimately associated with the Beings we call Spirits of Movement or Mights and those above them in the second Hierarchy, the Spirits of Wisdom or Dominions. These Beings were of special interest to them. The spiritual Beings of lower rank were, on the other hand, Beings whose domain they had already shared in former times and who therefore were no longer of particular importance to them. Thus they looked up to what later on they called the sum-total of the Spirits of Movement and of the Spirits of Wisdom, to that which was later characterized by the Greek expressions Dynamis and Kyriotetes. They beheld again these Beings and called them "Mula-prakriti", the sum-total of the Spirits of Movement, and "Maha-purusha", the sum-total of the Spirits of Wisdom, that which lives as if in a spiritual unity. They could attain to this vision because those who belonged to this people became ego-conscious at such a late stage of development. They had already undergone what the later peoples still had to experience through their 'I'.

The peoples belonging to the ancient Persian civilization were less highly developed. Their development was such that through their peculiar cognitive capacity, and through the awakening of their 'I' at a lower stage of evolution, they looked to the Powers or Spirits of Form. With these they were specially familiar; they could understand them to some extent and they were particularly interested in them. The peoples belonging to the Persian communities awakened to ego-consciousness one stage lower than the Indians, but it was a stage which the peoples of the West still had to reach. Hence the Persians were conversant with the Powers or Spirits of Form, known collectively as the 'Amshaspands''. They were the radiations which we know as Spirits of Form or Powers and which, from their point of view, the peoples of the Persian civilization were specially fitted to perceive clairvoyantly.

We then come to the Chaldean peoples. They were already aware of the Primal Forces, the directing Time Spirits, the Spirits of Personality. Now the peoples of the Graeco-Latin age also had a certain consciousness of these Primal Forces or Spirits of Personality, but in a different form. In their case there was an additional factor which may help to clarify our understanding. The Greeks were nearer to the Germanic peoples. They became ego-conscious at a higher stage than the Germanic-Nordic peoples. The working of the Angels and the Archangels in the human soul which the Northern peoples still experienced was no longer directly experienced by the Graeco-Latin peoples, though they still had a distinct recollection of it. The difference between the Germanic and Graeco-Latin peoples is that the latter still preserved a memory of the participation of Angels and Archangels in the development of their soul-life. On the whole they had no clear recollection of this stage for they were still in a state of diminished consciousness. But now in clairvoyant memory they recalled this experience quite distinctly. The creation of this whole world, the working of the Angels and Archangels, both normal and abnormal, in the human soul was known to the Greeks. They preserved in their souls vivid memory-pictures of what they had experienced. Now memory is much clearer, takes on sharper outlines than the immediate experiences of the present moment. It is no longer so fresh, no longer so youthful; memory or recollection has sharper contours, sharper

9—MOFS

outlines. Greek mythology is a memory-picture in bold, clear outlines of the influence or positive activity of the Angels and Archangels upon the human soul. If we do not approach Greek mythology in this way, if we simply compare Greek names with other names in the various mythologies, if we do not take into account the influence of special forces, nor understand the significance of the figures that appear as Apollo and Minerva and so on, then we are making a superficial study of comparative religion; we are only comparing externals. The manner or mode of perception in those days is the important point.

When we have grasped this, we realize that Greek mythology was built up from conscious memories. The Egyptians and Chaldeans had only a dim recollection of the activity of the Angels and Archangels, but they were able to perceive the world of Primal Forces. It seemed as if they were beginning to lose the memory of Angelic beings. Persian mythology, on the other hand, had completely forgotten the world of the Angels or Archangels, but at the same time men were able to look into the world of the Powers or Spirits of Form. That which is to be found in Greek mythology had been forgotten by the Persians and totally forgotten by the Indians. When they looked into the Akashic Record they perceived again the entire sequence of events of the earlier epochs and created pictures of the earlier events out of their knowledge which however was divine knowledge which they owed to more highly developed spiritual powers. This also helps to explain the great difficulty which the peoples of the East experienced in understanding the spiritual life of the West and that superior attitude which they adopted towards the spiritual life of the West. They are prepared to accept the materialistic civilization of the West, but the spiritual culture of the West— unless they come to it indirectly through Spiritual Science— remains more or less closed to them. They had already reached a high stage of evolution at a time when Christ Jesus had not yet descended upon Earth. He only incarnated in the fourth post-Atlantean epoch. That is an event which could no longer be grasped with the forces which the Indian people had developed. In order to apprehend the coming of Christ one needed faculties belonging to a less lofty station of the 'I'—a dwelling of the 'I' in more humble forces of the human soul.

The Teutonic peoples not only preserved a memory of the working of the Angels and Archangels into the soul of man, but even at the time when Christ Jesus walked upon Earth were aware that they were still subject to these influences and that they participated in the activity of the Angels and Archangels who were still active in their souls. When they underwent these inner experiences of the soul the Graeco-Latin peoples recalled something which they had gone through in former times. The Germanic peoples responded to these experiences more personally. Their ego had awakened at the stage of existence when the Folk Spirits and those spiritual Beings who were still subject to the Folk Spirits were still active in their souls; hence these peoples were nearest to the events that took place in old Atlantis.

In old Atlantis man beheld the spiritual Powers and spoke of a kind of unity of the Godhead, because he enjoyed direct perception into the old primeval states of human evolution. At that time one could still perceive the dominion of the Spirits of Wisdom and of the Spirits of Movement, a dominion which the Indians of a later epoch perceived again in the Akashic Records. These Germanic peoples of the West had raised themselves one stage above this level of perception, so that they experienced directly the transition from the old perception to the new. They perceived an active weaving of real spiritual powers at a time when the ego was not yet awake. But at the same time they saw the gradual awakening of the 'I' and the penetration of man's soul by the Angels and Archangels. They were aware of this direct transition. They preserved a clairvoyant memory of an earlier weaving life, when everything was seen through the dim mists of Atlantis and when, from out of this sea of mist, there emerged what we have come to know as the divine-spiritual Beings immediately above man. The old Gods, however, who were active before the Gods intervened in the life of the human soul, and who could now be seen and with whom men felt themselves to be united, those divine Beings who were active in the very far distant past at the time of old Atlantis, were called the Vanir. After Atlantis men saw the weaving of the Angels and

Archangels whom they called the Aesir. They were the Beings
who as Angels and Archangels were concerned with the 'I' of
man which then awoke at an elementary level. These Beings took
over the leadership of the Germanic peoples. What the other
peoples of the East had "slept through", namely, the perception
of how the soul, the inner life, was gradually developed by means
of the various forces which were bestowed upon it by the normal
and abnormal Angels and Archangels, this had to be experienced
by the peoples of Europe beginning from the lowest stage. They
had to be fully conscious in order that these soul-forces might
gradually develop.

Thus Nordic man perceived the figures of the Gods, the
divine Beings working directly upon his soul; he saw the human
soul wresting its way out of the Cosmos. This was direct experience
to him. He did not recall in retrospect how the souls of men had
been 'in-formed' into their bodies; rather did he see all this as
an immediate and present happening. He was there with his own
ego; he was a conscious witness of it. Even until the eighth, ninth
and tenth centuries A.D. he retained this feeling, this understanding of how the forces of the soul are gradually formed and
crystallized into the body. In the first place he beheld the Archangelic Beings who worked in his soul and endowed him with his
psychic potentialities, and the greatest of these Archangels was
Wotan or Odin.* He saw him at work upon his soul and he saw
how he worked into his soul. How did he perceive Wotan or Odin?
Who or what was he? In what form did Nordic man learn to love
Odin and above all to understand him? He learned to recognize
him as one of those Archangels who in the past had decided to
renounce their development to higher stages. He came to know
Odin as one of the abnormal Archangels, as one of the great
figures of renunciation in ancient times, who had assumed
the office of Archangel when they took upon themselves the
important task of working into the souls of men. Nordic man
experienced the activity of Odin at a time when he was still in the
process of giving the gift of language to the incarnating soul of
man. The manner in which Odin himself worked upon his
peoples in order to endow them with language has survived in a

*See Appendix.

remarkable way. It was described as a Divine Initiation. The means by which Odin acquired the power to give the gift of language to the Teutonic peoples is described as follows: before acquiring this capacity Odin had undergone Initiation by drinking at the spring of Mimir the magic draught of the Gods, that magic draught which once upon a time in the primeval past had been the draught of the Giants. This draught embodied not merely a generalized form of wisdom, but represented the wisdom that lives directly in the spoken sounds of speech. At his Initiation Odin won power over that wisdom which lives in sound. He learned how to make use of it when he underwent a long Initiation which lasted nine days and from which he was then released by Mimir, the ancient bearer of wisdom. Thus Odin became Lord of the power of language. This explains why the later saga traces the language of the bards or skalds back to Odin. Runic lore which in olden times was thought to be much more closely related to language than later literature and letters was also traced back to Odin. Therefore the manner in which the soul, indirectly through the etheric body, and interpenetrating the physical body, acquired the power of speech through the appropriate Archangel is expressed in the wonderful stories about Odin.

Similar Archangels are to be found amongst the companions of Odin: Hönir who gave the power of thought and Lodur who gave that which is intimately connected with race, namely pigmentation and the character of the blood. These two Beings, therefore, are Archangels more in the normal line. In Vili and Ve, on the other hand, we have Archangels of abnormal development. They are Beings who work more in the inner life, in the hidden recesses of the soul, as I pointed out in the last lecture. But an ego which is itself at an abnormal stage of evolution when it witnesses the cultivation of the subordinate forces of the human soul, feels itself to be intimately related to an abnormal Archangel. Odin, therefore, is not regarded as an abnormal Archangel, but rather as the kind of Archangel whose renunciation is akin to that of the Western peoples who are more aware that their inner development had been deferred, whereas the Eastern peoples by-passed certain stages of their psychic development until they awakened to ego-consciousness. Hence there lives especially in the soul of the Teutonic peoples all that is associated with the Archangelic forces of Odin stirring in the primitive depths of the human soul.

When we stated that the Angels are responsible for transmitting to the individual human beings the achievements of the Archangels, so also an 'I' which awakens at such an elementary level of soul-life is particularly concerned in seeing that the intentions of the Archangels are communicated to that ego. Hence Germanic-Nordic man has an interest in an Angel-being who is endowed with special power, but who at the same time is closely related to the single human being and his individuality. And that Being is Thor.* We can only recognize Thor when we see in him a Being who could have risen to far higher rank had he followed the normal course of evolution, but who renounced advancement comparatively early and remained at the stage of a Angel in order that, at the time when man awoke to ego-consciousness in the course of his soul's evolution, he could become the guiding Spirit in the spiritual life of the Teutonic peoples. What gives the immediate feeling that Thor is related to the individual human ego is that what was to be transmitted to every individual 'I' from the spiritual world could, in fact, be transmitted. If we bear this in mind we shall also understand more clearly the fragmentary information that has come down to us. It is important to have a right understanding of these individual Gods. Germanic-Nordic man perceived and himself experienced this imprinting of the soul in the body. He witnessed the integration of the ego into the body and the birth of ego-consciousness.

Now we know that the ego is incarnated in the pulsation of our blood and that everything within has its counterpart without, that everything microcosmic has its parallel in the macrocosmic. The work of Odin who gave speech and Runic wisdom, who worked indirectly through the breathing, has its counterpart in the movement of the wind in the macrocosm. The regular inhalation of the air through our respiratory organs which transform the air into words and speech corresponds to the movements and currents of the wind in the macrocosm outside. Just as we feel within ourselves the power of Odin in the trans-

*See Appendix.

formation of air into words, so too we must perceive his presence
and activity in the ambient winds. But those who still preserved
a certain degree of clairvoyance really saw the presence of
Odin everywhere in the cosmic element of the air, saw how he
formed speech by means of his breath. This Nordic man perceived as a unity. Just as that which lives in us and organizes our
speech—that is to say, in the form in which speech existed amongst
the Nordic peoples—penetrates into the ego and sets the blood
pulsating so too the inner organization of speech in man finds
its parallel in the macrocosm in thunder and lightning. The
gift of speech precedes the birth of the ego in man. Hence the 'I'
is everywhere felt to be the son of Odin to whom we owe the
gift of speech. Thor plays an active part in the implanting of the
individual ego, and in the microcosm the pulsation of the blood
corresponds to the thunder and lightning in the macrocosm.
Thus, in the macrocosm, the parallel to the pulsation of the blood
in man is the thunder and lightning in the sighing winds and the
weaving clouds. Germanic-Nordic man sees this clairvoyantly as a
unity; he perceives that the soughing of the wind and the
flashing of the lightning are intimately related to the breathing.
He sees how the air he inhales passes into the blood-stream and
sets the 'I' pulsating. Today this is looked upon as a physical
process, but to Germanic-Nordic man it was an astral experience.
He felt the kinship of the inner fire of the blood and of outer
lightning. He felt the pulse-beat in his blood and knew it to be
the pulse-beat of the 'I'. He was aware of this inner pulsation
and knew that it would recur. But he paid no heed to the external
physical process. All this was seen clairvoyantly. He felt that it
was the deed of Thor which caused the pulse to beat and made
the blood return again and again to the same source. He felt the
Thor-force in his 'I' as the hammer of Thor returning ever and
again into his hand; he felt the power of one of the mightiest
Angels who had ever been honoured or revered, because he was
a mighty Being who was seen to have remained behind at the
Angel stage.

The way in which the spiritual force holds together the physical
body is described in the Teutonic mythology where it says that
the 'I' is that which holds together the soul and body in the

formative stage. Germanic-Nordic man sees the weaving of the body and soul from within, and in later years he still understands how, originating in the astral, his inner life becomes integrated, how the inner answers, so to speak, to the outer. He could still respond when he learned from the Initiates that man was built out of the Cosmos. He was able to look back to earlier stages, to what had been told him about the events which reflected the relationship between the Angels and the Archangels, to those earlier stages when man was born out of the macrocosm in physical-spiritual form. He was able to perceive how the individual was built up out of the macrocosm and how he was an integral part of it. He sought in the macrocosm for those occurrences which are reflected in the microcosm. He could distinguish in the human microcosm, the microcosmic North, the cool realm where human thoughts are woven and whence the body is supplied with the twelve cranial nerves. He sees the weaving spirit in what he calls Nebelheim or Niflheim; he sees the twelve rivers which converge to form physically the twelve cranial nerves. He sees how the forces that issue from the microcosmic South, from the human heart, counteract the forces from above. He looks for them outside in the macrocosm and understands when he is told that they are called Muspelheim. Thus, even in the Christian era, it was still possible for him to comprehend the microcosm in terms of the whole macrocosm. And one could go back further still and show him how man gradually originated out of the macrocosm as extract of the whole world. He was able to look back into that time and he could understand that these events have a long ancestry, which he himself still sees as a working of the Angels and Archangels into his soul. He realizes that these events have a long ancestry and the conceptions he thus acquires we encounter in the old Teutonic Genesis, as the origin of mankind out of the entire macrocosm.

From Ginnungagap, the primeval abyss of Teutonic mythology, a new Earth emerges after having passed through the three earlier incarnations of Old Saturn, Old Sun, and Old Moon. The emergent world without form and void comes forth again out of Pralaya where the kingdoms of nature are not yet differentiated and men are still undivided and completely spiritual beings. It was then clear to Nordic man how the later conditions have developed out of this original abyss.

Now it is interesting to see how the events of those times are portrayed in Teutonic mythology in the form of imaginative pictures, events which we in our anthroposophical teachings describe in more sophisticated terms, using concepts in place of images. In Anthroposophy we are given a description of the events which took place when the Sun and Moon were still united, of the separation of the Moon and of the evolutionary transition to the later "Riesenheim". Everything which existed during the Atlantean epoch is described as a continuation of earlier epochs and as the particular concern of the Teutonic or Germanic people.

Today I only wanted to give an idea of how the Germanic peoples awakened to the ego while still at an elementary stage of evolution and how Nordic man perceived in full consciousness the Folk Soul, the soul of Thor and so on. I wanted to show how, as an ego-being, he was able to respond immediately to the inweaving of still higher Beings who, however, come from an entirely different realm from those we find among the Eastern peoples.

Tomorrow we shall attempt to explore the lesser known branches of Teutonic mythology. We shall discover how they are harbingers of that which dwells in the Folk Souls and we shall see what is the nature of our Western Folk Souls.

LECTURE NINE

Loki—Hödur and Baldur—Twilight of the Gods.

Those members of the audience who wish to analyse from a philosophical point of view my lecture of yesterday might meet perhaps with difficulties, apparent difficulties, because they will have heard in the course of earlier talks on similar themes that the purpose of our entire post-Atlantean epoch and even of the later stages of Atlantean evolution was to develop gradually the human ego and bring it to fuller consciousness. In this context I have indicated that the members of the ancient Indian civilization who had been able in Atlantis to perceive the spiritual world by means of the old clairvoyance still prevalent at that time were in some respects the very first who experienced an immediate transition from this clairvoyant state to a consciousness of the physical world. Their reaction to this physical world was such that the whole of this post-Atlantean age was pervaded by the feeling that true reality was to be found in the spiritual world, whilst the phenomenal world was merely Maya or illusion. Now I pointed out in our last lecture—and the facts confirm this—that the members of this ancient Indian civilization had to some extent undergone a rich soul-development and that they had achieved this high level whilst their ego was more or less asleep, that is to say, that they only awoke to ego-consciousness after they had already reached maturity of soul-development.

What, then, was the destiny of these Indian peoples meanwhile? For the Indian peoples must have experienced their entire soul-development in a wholly different manner from the European and especially the Germanic peoples who were ego-conscious whilst their capacities were gradually evolving and who were conscious of the divine-spiritual power working into their souls. You may possibly find it difficult to reconcile my statements in yesterday's lecture if you were to reflect upon that lecture philosophically. For those who wish to analyse that lecture, not from a disinterested point of view, but from a philosophical angle, I must add something in parenthesis by way of explanation.

The apparent contradiction will resolve itself at once if you recall that cognition of the ego is totally different from other forms of cognition. If the ego "knows" any other object or other human being distinct from itself, then in the act of cognition one is really dealing with two factors, with the knower, the cognizing agent, and the known. In the formal act of cognition it is irrelevant whether that which is known is human being, animal, tree or stone. But it is a different matter when the ego knows itself, for then the knower and the known are one, subject and object of cognition are the same. It is important to realize that in human evolution, in the development of the individual, these two modes of cognition are distinct. Those who had developed the mature Indian culture in the post-Atlantean epoch, developed the 'I' subjectively as the knower, a cognizing agent, and this subjective enhancement of the 'I' within the human soul may exist for a long time before man acquires the power to see the 'I' objectively as an entity. On the other hand, the European peoples developed comparatively early, whilst they still preserved the old clairvoyance, the power to see the 'I' objectively, that is to say, in their clairvoyant field of vision they perceived the 'I' as an entity amongst other entities. If you distinguish carefully between these modes of perception your philosophical problems will be solved and those of Spiritual Science too, if you approach them in the right way. If you wish me to express it in philosophical terms: the Indian culture exhibits a soul which reached the full flowering of the subjective 'I' long before the objective 'I' was developed. The Teutonic peoples developed the perception of the 'I' long before they became conscious of the real inner striving towards the 'I'. Clairvoyantly they saw the dawning of their ego in an imaginative picture. In the astral world around them they had long seen the 'I' objectively amongst the other beings whom they perceived clairvoyantly. Thus we must conceive of this antithesis in a purely formal manner; then we shall also comprehend why Europe in particular was destined to associate this 'I' of man with the other higher Beings, the Angels and Archangels, in the way I pointed out yesterday in relation to mythology.

If you bear this in mind you will realize that Europe was destined to relate the ego in a multiplicity of ways to the world perceptible to the senses and that the ego, the fundamental essence of the human being, can enter into the most varied relationship with the external world. Formerly, before man was aware of his ego, before he perceived it, these relationships were determined for him by the higher Beings and he himself remained a passive instrument. His relationship to the external world was a purely instinctive one. The decisive factor in the development of the ego is that it should progressively determine its relationship to the external world. Substantially it was the task of the European nations to determine in some way or other this relation of the 'I' to the whole world, and the guiding Folk Soul had, and still has the task of directing European man how to bring his 'I' into relation with the external world, with other egos and with the world of spiritual Beings, so that on the whole it was within European civilization that one first began to speak of the relationship of the human ego to the surrounding universe. Hence the completely different atmosphere in the old Indian cosmology from that prevailing in the mythological culture of Europe. In the East everything is impersonal, and, above all, one is required to adopt a passive attitude towards knowledge, to suppress the ego in order to become merged in Brahma and to find Atman within oneself. In the East, therefore, the primary objective is to lose one's identity and seek union with the Absolute. In Europe this human 'I' occupies a central place in human life in accordance with its original innate tendencies and with its progressive development in the course of evolution. In Europe, therefore, particular attention is given to seeing everything in relation to the 'I', to showing clairvoyantly the relationship of the 'I' to everything that had participated in the development of the 'I' in the course of earthly existence.

Now you all know that two opposing forces have participated in the development of terrestrial man who was destined gradually to acquire his 'I'. Ever since the Lemurian epoch Luciferic forces have imprinted themselves upon the inner being of man, upon his astral body. You know that these forces made man's inner life the focal point of attack by infiltrating into his desires, impulses and passions. In consequence, man benefitted in two ways: he was able to become a free and independent being, to be fired with enthusiasm for what he thinks, feels and wills, whereas in relation to his own affairs he was guided by divine-spiritual Beings. But on the other hand, through the Luciferic powers, man had to accept the possibility of falling into evil through his passions, emotions and desires. Lucifer, therefore, is omnipresent in our Earth-existence and finds his point of attack in the inner being of man, in the play of the human astral. Where the astral has been integrated with the ego, the ego too has been permeated by the Luciferic power. When therefore we speak of Lucifer, we are speaking of that which has thrust man down deeper into material, sensory existence than would have been the case without that influence. Thus to the Luciferic powers we owe the most precious boon to man, namely, freedom, and, at the same time a dangerous legacy, the possibility of evil.

But we also know that because these Luciferic powers had intervened in the entire constitution of human nature, other powers were able to enter later on, which could not have done so had not Lucifer first invaded the human organism. Man would see the world differently if he had not fallen under the influence of Lucifer and his followers, if he had not been obliged to submit to the influence of another power after he had opened himself to the invasion of a Luciferic power. Ahriman approached from outside and penetrated into the vast arena of the phenomenal world surrounding man, so that the Ahrimanic influence is therefore a consequence of the Luciferic influence. Lucifer, as it were, takes possession of man from within and in consequence he is the victim of Ahriman who works from without.

The spiritual science of all ages that is familiar with the real facts, speaks of both Luciferic and Ahrimanic powers. It will seem very remarkable to you that the various peoples who express these views in the form of mythology are not always aware of Lucifer and Ahriman to the same extent. For instance, there is no clear awareness of this in a religious conception built up out of the whole Semitic tradition as embodied in the Old Testament. Only a certain consciousness of the Luciferic influence can be found there. You will find evidence for this in the Old Testament account of the Serpent which is simply a picture of Lucifer. And this shows that there was a clear realization that Lucifer played a part in evolution, a realization that is undeniably present in all traditions associated with the Bible. But they do not betray an awareness of the Ahrimanic influence to the same extent; that is only to be found where spiritual science is taught. Therefore the Gospel writers have taken this into account. You will find—for at the time when the Gospels were written the word 'devil' or 'daimon' was borrowed from the Greek—that St Mark's Gospel does not speak of the temptation of Jesus, but of a devil tempting Him; but in all references to Ahriman the word Satan is used. But who notices the important difference between these descriptions in the Gospel of St. Mark and that of St. Matthew? Exoterically these fine distinctions are not heeded at all, nor is this difference noted in external traditions.

This difference is very apparent in the contrast between India and Persia and is strikingly illustrated at a certain moment in history. The Persians were less subject to the Luciferic influence than the Ahrimanic. It was in Persia in particular that men wrestled with the powers which give us an external, false picture of the world and which surround us with the forces of darkness, i.e. that which is concerned with man's relation to the external world. Ahriman is known chiefly as an opponent of the Good and as an enemy of the Light. What is the explanation of this? The explanation is that in the second post-Atlantean epoch man developed his perception of the external world. Remember that the task of Zoroaster was to reveal the Sun Spirit, the Spirit of Light. He has first to show that this world is compounded of Light and the Spirit of Darkness who dims our consciousness of the external world. The Persian aims primarily at the conquest of Ahriman and strives to unite himself with the Children of Light, the Spirits who are here the dominant Powers. He is organized for activity in the external world; hence he has his Ahuras or Asuras. It is, on the other hand, dangerous for the followers of the Persian religion to look inwards, to follow the inward path. Where the Luciferic powers are lurking he will not allow himself to become aware of the good powers which are present there: he senses danger. He directs his gaze outwards and believes the Asuras of Light to be in opposition to the Asuras of Darkness.

At this time the Indians pursued exactly the opposite course. They lived in a period when they endeavoured to raise themselves into the higher spheres by inner contemplation. They sought salvation by uniting themselves with the forces of inner vision. It was dangerous, they felt, to look out into the external world where they might have to wrestle with Ahriman. They feared the external world and regarded it as dangerous. Whereas the Persians eschewed the Devas, the Indians looked up to them and wanted to work in their domain. But the Persians turned away and avoided the region where the battle against Lucifer had to be fought.

Search as you will through the many different mythologies and conceptions of the world, in none of them will you find such a clear and profound awareness of the fact that there are two influences at work on man as in Teutonic mythology. As Nordic man was still clairvoyant, he really saw these two powers and took up a position midway between them. He said to himself: In the course of his evolution man has seen the advent of certain powers which penetrated into his inner being and worked upon his astral body; they operated from without. And because he was destined to develop the 'I', to achieve independence, he sensed not merely the possibility of evil, but, in these powers which permeated his astral body in order to bring freedom and independence, he felt above all the aspiration to freedom. He felt, one might say, the rebellious element manifesting itself in these forces. He felt the presence of the Luciferic element in the power which in these Scandinavian and Germanic regions even then still participated in the creation of races, in that it gave man his external form and pigmentation and made him an independent, active being in the world. With his clairvoyance Nordic man felt Lucifer to be primarily that which makes man a free being, one who is not prepared to submit passively to random external powers, but is solid and reliant and is determined to act independently. Nordic man felt this Luciferic influence to be beneficial.

But he now realized that something else stemmed from this influence. Lucifer conceals himself behind the figure of Loki who has a remarkably irridescent form. Because Nordic man could perceive the reality, he saw that the thoughts of the freedom and independence of man can be traced to Loki. Through the old clairvoyance, however, he was also aware that that which repeatedly drags man down through his desires and actions and causes him to suffer a greater deterioration of his whole being than would have befallen him had he devoted himself to Odin and the Aesir, is to be attributed to the influence of Loki. And now he felt the awful grandeur of this Teutonic mythology; he felt with passionate conviction that which will only return gradually to the consciousness of man through Spiritual Science.

How, then, does the Luciferic influence act? It penetrates into the astral body and thus is able to work upon all the three members of man, upon his astral, etheric and physical bodies. At the present day one can only give indications of this Luciferic influence outside the Anthroposophical Society. What you will come to understand more and more clearly is that the Luciferic influence makes itself felt in three different ways: in the astral body, in the etheric body, and in the physical body of man.

It begets in the etheric body the urge to falsehood and lying. Lies and falsehood are not limited to the inner life of man. In the astral body, the vehicle of man's inner life, the self is permeated with a Luciferic influence which takes the form of selfishness. The etheric body is inwardly motivated by the impulse to be untruthful and is thus disposed to lying. In the physical body the Luciferic influence begets sickness and death. That will be easily understood by those who were present at my last series of lectures.* I should like to emphasize once again that the signs and symptoms of physical death are karmically connected with the Luciferic influence. To recapitulate again briefly: Lucifer begets in the astral body selfishness, in the etheric body lying and falsehood, and in the physical body sickness and death.

*The Manifestations of Karma. Eleven lectures given in Hamburg, May 1910 (Rudolf Steiner Press).

Of course the materialists of the present day will be greatly surprised to learn that Spiritual Science attributes sickness and death to a Luciferic influence. But this too is connected with Karma. But for the Luciferic influence man would never have known sickness and death. The karmic effect of this influence is that man is more deeply immersed in corporeality and, on the other hand, the penalty for this is sickness and death.

We may say that when the Luciferic influence entered into man, the physical, etheric and astral bodies became a prey to sickness and death, lying, falsehood and selfishness. I should like to draw your attention to the fact that the materialistic scientists of today assign death in the human being or in the animal or plant to the same cause. They fail to realize that one external appearance may resemble another and yet may originate from totally different causes.

An external situation may arise from a variety of causes. The death of an animal does not supervene from the same cause as the death of a man, although externally it gives the same impression.

It would take too long to provide an epistemological proof of these things. I only wish to state here that the scientific view of causality is sadly mistaken. We meet with mistakes such as these, which arise from muddled thinking, at almost every turn. Imagine the case of a man who climbs onto a roof, falls down, is mortally injured and is picked up dead. What would be more natural than to say: "The man fell down, was mortally injured and died of his injuries." But there might have been a totally different explanation. The man might have had a stroke whilst on the roof and have fallen down while already dead. The injuries might have been caused by the fall, so that externally this case might appear the same as the one described before, but death would have supervened from an entirely different cause.

This is a very crude example, but scientists are very frequently guilty of this kind of mistake. Externally the real facts may often be exactly the same: the inner causes may be completely different.

We claim, then, from the results of spiritual-scientific investigation that the Luciferic influence begets in the astral

10—MOFS * *

body selfishness, in the etheric body lying and falsehood and in the physical body sickness and death. Now what would the Teutonic mythology have had to say if it had been obliged to ascribe this threefold influence to Loki, to Lucifer? It would have had to say that Loki has three offspring. The first, the one who begets selfishness, is the Midgard Snake through whom is expressed the influence of the Luciferic spirit on the astral body. The second is that which falsifies human knowledge. In man, on the physical plane, this consists in those things of the mind which do not accord with the external world. It is that which has no validity there. To Nordic man who lived more on the astral plane, that which to us is an illusion manifested itself at once as an astral being and lived as such upon the astral plane. The expression for everything that implied darkening of the light of truth, false perspective, was some kind of animal; and here in the North it was chiefly the Fenris Wolf. This second animal is Loki's influence on the etheric body to which man owes his inner inclination to deceive himself, to think incorrectly about things; that is to say, the objects in the external world do not appear to him in true perspective. This was generally expressed in the old Teutonic mythology in the form of a wolf. That is the astral form for lying and falsehood which proceeds from inner impulse.

Where man is related to the external world Lucifer confronts Ahriman, so that the infiltration of error into his knowledge—even into his clairvoyant knowledge—all illusion and maya, is the consequence of the tendency to falsehood which is active there. The Fenris Wolf represents the configuration surrounding man because he does not see things in their true form. Whenever the ancient Teutons experienced the darkening of the light of truth, they spoke of a wolf. This permeates the whole of Nordic consciousness and you will find that this image is used in this sense even in relation to external facts.

When the ancient Teutons wanted to explain what they saw during an eclipse of the Sun—in the epoch of the old clairvoyance of course, man saw very differently from the man of today who uses a telescope—they chose the image of a wolf pursuing the Sun and who, the moment he overtakes it, causes an eclipse. This agrees perfectly with the facts. This terminology is an integral part of the grandeur, that awful grandeur peculiar to Teutonic mythology. I can only give indications here, but if it were possible to speak for weeks on end upon this Teutonic mythology, you would then see how this is universally applied in the representations of Teutonic mythology. This is because Teutonic mythology is a consequence of the old clairvoyance into which the 'I' plays everywhere.

Materialists of today will reply that this is pure superstition, that there is no wolf in pursuit of the Sun. The old imaginative Nordic man sees these facts in the form of pictures and I could perhaps enumerate many so-called scientific truths which contain more Ahrimanic influence, a greater degree of error, than the corresponding astral perception which describes the wolf in pursuit of the Sun. That an eclipse occurs because the Moon interposes itself between the Earth and the Sun seems to the occultist to betray a mind that is even more superstitious. From the external point of view the explanation of the eclipse is perfectly correct, just as the case of the wolf is perfectly correct from the astral point of view. In fact the astral view is more correct than the one you will find in modern text-books which is even more subject to error. If at some future time man is prepared to accept the real facts instead of this external explanation, he will find that the Teutonic myth is correct. I am aware that I am saying something which is ridiculously absurd in the eyes of contemporary man, but I know too that in anthroposophical circles one is already sufficiently advanced to be in a position to show in which respects the physical view of the world is most influenced by maya, deception or illusion.

Let us now turn to the influence of Loki on the physical body. His third offspring is Hel, who begets sickness and death. Thus the figures Hel, the Fenris Wolf and the Midgard Snake are wonderful representations of the influence of Loki or Lucifer in the form in which his influence was perceived by the old dreamlike clairvoyance. If we were to follow out the whole history of Loki we should everywhere find that these things throw light upon the matter, down to the smallest details. But we must clearly understand that what the clairvoyant sees are not allegories, but real Beings.

Selfishness - Midgard Snake

Luciferic Influence

Astral Body
Ether Body   *Untruthfulness - Fenris Wolf*
Phys. Body

Illness - Death - Hel

Now Nordic man was not only aware of Loki, of the Luciferic influence, but also of the influence of Ahriman which was the polar opposite, and he knew too that involvement in the Ahrimanic influence was a consequence of the Luciferic influence. If you now look back to the time when man did not apprehend the world through sensory perception but contemplated it with the old clairvoyance, you will find that this myth has been developed in response to this clairvoyance. What does the myth say? Man has succumbed to the influence of Loki, and this is expressed in the activity of the Midgard Snake, the Fenris Wolf and Hel. The effect was such that man's perception, his clear, luminous vision into the spiritual world, became dimmed, because the Luciferic influence increasingly asserted itself. At that time, when this view developed, man alternated between a consciousness that was able to see into the spiritual world and a consciousness that was directed to the physical plane, just as we normally alternate between waking and sleeping. When he gazed into the spiritual world he looked into the world out of which he was born. The essential point is that the myth had its source in the clairvoyant consciousness. But human consciousness consisted in this alteration between insight into, and loss of insight into the spiritual world. When man lived in a condition of dreamlike consciousness he saw into the spiritual world. When in a condition of waking consciousness, he was blind to it. Thus he alternated between the conditions of blindness to, and insight into, the spiritual world. His consciousness alternated just as a certain Cosmic Being alternated between the blind Hödur and the clairvoyant Baldur, who could see into the spiritual world. Thus man was predisposed to receive Baldur's influence and he would have developed in accordance with this influence if he had not been subject to Loki's influence. It was Loki's responsibility, however, that the Hödur nature overcame the Baldur nature. This is expressed by Loki bringing the mistletoe, with which the blind Hödur kills Baldur, the one who sees.

Loki therefore is the destructive power, like Lucifer who drove man into the arms of Ahriman. In so far as man submits to the blind Hödur, the old clairvoyant vision is extinguished. That is the slaying of Baldur. This is felt by Nordic man as the gradual extinction of the Baldur power, the loss of the vision into the spiritual world. Thus, in the loss of clairvoyance, Nordic man felt that by the death of Baldur Loki had extinguished clairvoyance and that henceforth he was powerless to revive this erstwhile clairvoyance. Thus one of the greatest historical events, the gradual loss of the old, unclouded knowledge is expressed in the myth of Baldur, Hödur and Loki. On the one hand, therefore, we have Loki with his kinsmen, the three Beings, and on the other, the tragic slaying of Baldur.

Thus, in Teutonic mythology, is reflected that which we can derive from Spiritual Science: the twofold influence—the Luciferic and the Ahrimanic. It is this which Spiritual Science always seeks to present to you as an illustration of the clairvoyant knowledge of ancient times and as a development of the myth out of the old clairvoyance which then gradually began to disappear.

It would take us too far if we were to pursue this subject further. But even in the broad outline I have presented to you, you can feel the awful grandeur of this myth, which is unsurpassed, because no other mythology adheres so closely to the old clairvoyant condition. Greek mythology is only a memory of something experienced in former times, expressed in sculptural form. Greek mythology has no longer that direct association with the facts which one finds in Teutonic mythology. It is more sophisticated, more mature, the figures show more clearly defined, more finished contours, and therefore appear markedly sculptural. They have lost the primitive simplicity of the earliest impressions. The old clairvoyance which had long vanished in the rest of Europe still survived in the North. Only slowly, step by step, has the perspective of man become limited to the picture of the physical world alone. Thus, at the time when Christianity began to spread abroad, that which is expressed in the Baldur myth, in the death of Baldur, had become true for the majority of men. There were, however, still a few who were able to perceive directly what Nordic man experienced clairvoyantly.

Thus for a long time there still existed the direct perception of the spiritual world, and because it was still so elemental and sprang so directly from clairvoyant experience, there still survived, when Christianity began to spread abroad, this conscious awareness of the spiritual world which was more developed in the Teutonic peoples than in any other. Then they felt that their erstwhile experiences of their original spiritual home were vanishing. And these spiritual experiences were lost when Nordic man received the consolations of Christianity. But Christianity did not offer him any direct vision. He had felt the fate of Baldur much too deeply to be able to console himself for this loss by exchanging Baldur for a God who had descended to the physical plane in order that the children of men who could only perceive on the physical plane, may also be allowed to rise to a consciousness of God. Unlike the peoples of the Near East the Northern peoples were unable to respond to the words: "Change your mental attitude, for the Kingdom of Heaven is at hand!" In Palestine where Christ was born, there existed only long-lost memories of the fact that once upon a time there had been an old clairvoyance. In the East, the Kali Yuga, the Dark Age, had already lasted for three thousand years, when men could no longer see into the spiritual world. But they always yearned for that world and have ever told of a world which man was once able to perceive spiritually. But it was a world which had now vanished from their sight. Hence they had experienced the spiritual world in a much more distant past than the men of the North, and they only knew from memory that the spiritual world had once been within reach. Hence the peoples of Asia Minor could well understand the words: "Change your mental attitude for the Kingdom of Heaven is at hand!" They could understand the words: "The Kingdom of

Heaven is nigh unto you even here upon the physical plane. Seek ye therefore the unique figure who will appear in the land of Palestine, seek ye the Messiah, the Incarnation of the Godhead, through whom you too will be able to find your relation to the Divine, even though you cannot raise yourself above the physical plane. Recognize that Figure in Palestine, know the Figure of Christ!" Those were the profound words of John the Baptist.

The Nordic man, of necessity, felt this differently; for a longer period of time he had experienced much more than the mere memory of a vision into the spiritual world. Hence there arose in him a thought of far-reaching importance, namely: this limitation to the outer physical plane, this darkening of spiritual sight, can only be an intermediate time. There must be a period of probation and man will have to discover what the physical world can teach him. This transition is necessary and he must therefore withdraw from the spiritual world. He must undergo the experience of the phenomenal world as a necessary training. But through this period of probation he will find his way back to that world whence he came. The vision of Baldur will be able to ensoul him again. In other words, the great truth which dawned in the course of the evolution of the Teutonic peoples that the world which was lost to clairvoyant vision would again become visible, he owed to the fact that man felt his sojourn on the physical plane to be a time of transition.

The Initiates had taught Nordic man that a change was taking place in the spiritual world during the intermediate time when he had lost the vision of the spiritual world and in consequence it would one day appear transformed. They explained this to him somewhat as follows: "Formerly you looked into the spiritual world and there you saw the Archangel of Speech, the Archangel of the Runes, Odin,* the Archangel of Respiration, and Thor, the Angel of Egohood. You were associated with them, and he who is sufficiently prepared will be able to enter the spiritual world again. But it will then appear different; other powers will have been added to it, and the spheres of power and the relationships of power of those old spiritual leaders of the human race

*See Appendix.

will have changed. You will, it is true, see into this world, but you will find it transformed."

What man will then see, the Initiates described to him as a vision of the future—the Vision that will one day appear to man when he is able to see into the spiritual world again, when he will see what has been the destiny of the old Gods and what was their relation to other powers. They described to him this vision of the future as seen by the Initiates when the Luciferic influence will to some extent override that which comes from the Gods and will, in its turn, be overcome. This was their vision of Ragnarok, the Twilight of the Gods. And again we shall see that all the events which were portrayed as future events could not, even down to the smallest details, be portrayed better or more aptly, nor in more fitting terminology than in the wonderful picture of the Twilight of the Gods. That is the occult background to the Saga of the Twilight of the Gods.

In what light, then, should man see himself? He should see himself as one who has received all that stems from earlier epochs as the origin and cause of his evolution. He should thoughtfully assimilate what he received as a gift from Odin, whilst feeling that he himself has undergone the ensuing evolution. He should receive into himself the teaching implanted in him by Odin. He should fight the good fight without delay. The Initiate, the Leader of the Esoteric School, makes that clear, particularly to Nordic man, by calling our attention to the divine-spiritual Being who appears to us so mysteriously, who in fact first plays a definite part in the Twilight of the Gods because he overcomes even that power by which Odin is at first overcome. In the Twilight of the Gods the rôle of Odin's avenger is a special rôle. When we understand this rôle we shall then perceive the wonderful connection between the native talents of the Teutonic peoples and our conception of our vision of the future. All this is expressed in a wonderful way, down to the smallest details, in the mighty vision of the Twilight of the Gods.

LECTURE TEN

The Mission of individual Peoples and Cultures
in the Past, Present and Future.
Solovieff.

Before we enlarge upon what will emerge from any further
elaboration of the significant image of the Twilight of the Gods,
it will be well to establish a firm foundation from which to
proceed. For we shall deal with the nature of the Germanic and
Scandinavian Folk Soul, and from the results of our investigation
describe it in greater detail. We shall discover how the whole
spiritual life of Europe works in concert, how the activity of the
various Folk Spirits has furthered the development of mankind
in the remote past, in the present and will continue to do so in the
future. Every single people, even isolated fragments of peoples,
have their special contribution to make to this great collective
task. You will realize from what has been said that, in certain
respects, the task, the mission of educating the 'I' through the
evolutionary stages of the human being, of shaping it and of
gradually developing it, devolved upon the Christian and post-
Christian cultures of Europe in particular. In primitive times, as
we have shown in the case of the Scandinavian and Germanic
peoples, the 'I' was revealed clairvoyantly to man. According
to tradition this 'I' was bestowed upon man by an Angelic
Being, Donar or Thor, who stands midway between man and
the Folk Soul. We have seen that the individual still felt himself to
be ego-less, devoid of personality; he looked upon the 'I' as a
gift from the spiritual world.

In the East, when the 'I' really awoke, it was not of course
experienced in the same way. There man had already reached
subjectively such a high degree of perfection that he did not
feel the 'I' as something extraneous, but as his own property. At
the time when man became ego-conscious in the East, Eastern

culture was already so far advanced that it was capable of gradually developing that finely-spun speculation, logic and wisdom which is reflected in Eastern wisdom. The East, therefore, no longer experienced the whole process of receiving the ego as if it were bestowed by a higher spiritual world through the instrumentality of a divine-spiritual Being such as Thor. That was the experience of Europe; hence the European felt this gradual unfolding of the individual 'I' as the emergence out of the Group Soul. The Germanic-Scandinavian man still felt himself attached to a Group Soul, to be a member of a closely knit unit or family, that he belonged to an integrated community. For this reason, nearly a hundred years after Christ, Tacitus could describe the Teutons of Central Europe as apparently belonging to separate tribes and yet as members of an organism, and belonging to the unity of the organism. Thus each individual still felt himself at that time to be a member of the tribal 'I'. He felt his individual 'I' gradually emerging from the tribal 'I' and he recognized in the God Thor the bestower of the 'I', the God who really endowed him with his individual 'I'. But at the same time he felt that this God was still united with the collective spirit of the tribe, with that which lives in the Group Soul. To this Group Soul was given the name "Sif". This is the name of the spouse of Thor. Sif is related linguistically to the word Sippe, kinship, although the relationship is veiled or concealed. Occultly, however, Sif signifies the Group Soul of the individual community from which the individual emerges. Sif is the Being who unites herself with the God of the individual 'I', with Thor, the bestower of the individual 'I'. The individual perceives Sif and Thor as the Beings who endowed him with his 'I'. It was in this way that Nordic man experienced them at a time when the peoples in other regions of Europe had already been given other tasks in preparing man's ego-development.

Each individual people had its appointed task; chief amongst them was that homogeneous group of peoples, that widely distributed folk community whom we know by the name of Celts. It was the responsibility of the ancient Celtic Folk Spirit, who, as we know from earlier lectures, was later given quite different tasks, to educate the still youthful 'I' of the peoples of

Europe. To this end it was necessary that the Celts themselves
should receive an education and instruction which was mediated
directly from the higher world. Hence it was entirely appropriate that through their Initiates, the Druid priests, the Celts
should transmit to other nations instruction received from
higher worlds and which they could not have acquired of themselves.

The whole of European culture is a legacy of the European
Mysteries. The progressive Folk Souls are always the leaders of
the collective culture of mankind as it unfolds. But at the time
when these European Folk Spirits enjoined upon men to act
more on their own initiative it was necessary that the Mysteries
should gradually withdraw. Hence with the withdrawal of the
Celtic element there followed a gradual withdrawal of the
Mysteries into more secret places. At the time of the ancient
Celts the Mysteries established a much more direct relationship
between the spiritual Beings and the people, because the 'I' was
still attached to the group-soul-life and yet the Celtic element
was to bring the gift of the 'I' to the other Germanic tribes. Thus
in the period preceding the evolution proper of the Northern
and Germanic peoples, the Mystery teachings could be given to
European civilization only by the ancient Celtic Mysteries. These
Mystery teachings allowed just so much to be revealed as was
necessary in order to establish a basis for the whole culture of
Europe. Now the most diverse Folk Souls and Folk Spirits were
able to draw nourishment from this old culture by mingling with
the widely diverse racial fragments, national communities and
folk elements, and they brought the 'I' into ever new situations
in order to nurture it, the 'I' which was struggling to free itself
from its attachment to the group-soul.

After the old Greek culture had to a certain extent reached
its high point in the fulfilment of its special mission, we see a
totally different aspect of this same mission in the spirit of ancient
Rome and its various stages of culture. We have already mentioned that the several post-Atlantean civilizations follow upon
one another in strict sequence. If we wish to have an overall
picture of the successive stages of post-Atlantean civilization we
may summarize them as follows: the old Indian culture worked

upon the human etheric body. Hence the remarkable wisdom and clairvoyant insight of the ancient Indian culture, because—after the development of special human capacities—it was a culture reflected in the human etheric body. We may envisage the ancient Indian culture somewhat as follows:

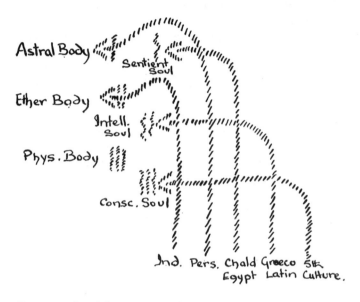

Between the Atlantean epoch and the later post-Atlantean epoch the Indian Folk Spirit developed to the full his inner soul-forces without developing ego-consciousness. He then returned to his activity in the etheric body. The essential element in the ancient Indian culture is that the ancient Indian was able to return again to the etheric body with his highly developed, highly refined faculties of soul and within that body he developed those marvellously delicate forces the later reflection of which we can still see in the Vedas, and in a still more refined form in the Vedanta philosophy. This was only possible because the Indian Folk Soul had achieved a high degree of development before it was conscious of the 'I', and this again at a time when man could perceive by means of the forces of the etheric body.

The Persian Folk Soul had not developed so far; its organ of perception was limited to the sentient body or astral body. The Egypto-Babylonian-Chaldean culture was again different. Here the organ of perception was the Sentient Soul; and the characteristic of the Egypto-Chaldean culture was the ability to work in the Sentient Soul. The Graeco-Latin Folk Spirit was related to the Intellectual or Mind-Soul in which he was active. He himself was only able to work upon this Intellectual Soul because the Intellectual Soul, in its turn, had a kind of psychic counterpart in the etheric body. But the form of cosmogony that now emerged in Greece was, to some extent, less real, less clear-cut; it had less the stamp of reality. Whilst the form of cognition in the ancient Indian culture was directly related to the activity of the etheric body, the Greek culture presented a blurred, pale, lifeless image of reality; as I have already said, it was like the memory of what these people had once experienced, like a memory reflected in their etheric body.

In the other peoples who followed the Greeks we are chiefly concerned with the use of the physical body for the progressive development of the Spiritual Soul (or Consciousness-Soul). Hence the Greek culture was a culture that we can only understand from within, if we realize that in this culture what is important in external experience is that which springs from the inner life of the Greeks. On the other hand, the peoples living more towards the West and the North had, under the guidance of their Folk Souls, to turn increasingly towards the external world, towards the phenomena of the physical plane, and to develop whatsoever has a part to play on that plane. This was the special task of the Northern and Germanic peoples which they alone could fulfil, because they still enjoyed the gift, the supremely important gift of the old clairvoyance which enabled them to see into the spiritual world and to incorporate the primeval spiritual experiences which were still vital in their souls into that which was to be established upon the physical plane.

There was one people who, at its later stage, no longer possessed this gift, who had not undergone such preliminary evolution and who had incarnated suddenly on the physical plane before the birth of the human 'I' and was only able therefore to attend to whatsoever furthered the development of this 'I' on the physical plane, to whatsoever was necessary for its well-being there under the guidance of its Folk Soul, its Archangel. This was the Roman people. Everything that the Roman people had to accomplish for the collective mission of Europe under the guidance of its Folk Spirit was directed to winning recognition for the 'I' of man. Hence the Roman people was able to develop human and social relationships. They were the founders of civil law and jurisprudence which are built up purely on the 'I'. The relation of human 'I' to human 'I' was the great question in the mission of the Roman people. The Western peoples whose civilizations grew out of the Roman civilization already possessed more of that which, coming from the Sentient Soul, Intellectual or Mind-Soul and from the Spiritual or Consciousness-Soul itself, fructifies the 'I' in some way and projects it outward into the world. Therefore all the mingling of races which external history records and which is found in the Italian and Iberian peninsulas, in France and Great Britain today, was necessary in order to develop the 'I' on the physical plane in accordance with the different nuances of the Sentient Soul, the Intellectual Soul and the Spiritual Soul. Such was the great mission of those peoples who gradually developed in the most diverse ways in Western Europe.

All the individual shades of culture, all the particular missions of the peoples of Western Europe can finally be explained by the fact that in the area of the Italian and Iberian peninsulas was to be developed that which could be formed in the 'I' through the impulses of the Sentient Soul. If you study the individual folk characters in their positive and negative aspects you will find that the peoples of the Italian and Iberian peninsulas reflect a peculiar fusion of the 'I' with the Sentient Soul. You will be able to understand, however, the peculiar characteristics of those peoples who, until recent times, lived on the soil of France, if you study the growth and fusion of the Intellectual Soul with the 'I'. The great world-wide achievements of a country such as Great Britain can be attributed to the fact that the impulse of the Spiritual Soul has penetrated into the human 'I'. With the world mission of the British Empire is also associated parliamentary forms of government and the founding of constitutional rights. The union of the Spiritual Soul with the human ego had not yet been realized inwardly. If you recognize how this union between the Spiritual Soul and the 'I' that was oriented outwards originated, you will find that the great historical conquests of the inhabitants of that island proceed from this impulse. You will also find that the establishment of parliamentary forms of government at once becomes comprehensible if one realizes that, in consequence of this, an impulse of the Spiritual Soul was to find expression on the plane of world-history.

Thus cultural diversities were a necessity, for the individual peoples had to be guided through the many stages of ego-development. If we had sufficient time to enlarge upon these matters we could find examples from history which show the ramifications of these basic forces and how they manifest in the most diverse ways. Thus the peculiar constitution of soul influenced the Western peoples who had not preserved the direct, original memory of the old clairvoyant insight into the spiritual world of former times. In the Germanic and Northern regions in later times, that which proceeded directly from a gradual, continuous evolution of the original clairvoyance with which the Sentient Soul had already been imbued, had to develop in a wholly different way. This accounts for that characteristic trait of inwardness which is only the after-effect of a clairvoyant insight experienced in a former age. The task of the Southern Germanic peoples lay primarily in the domain of the Spiritual Soul. The Graeco-Latin age had to develop the Intellectual Soul (or Mind-Soul). But not only this; it had also to include a wonderful development still working in from prehistoric times and imbued with clairvoyant insight. All this was then poured into the Spiritual Soul of the Central European and Scandinavian peoples and its after-effects lived on as an inner disposition of soul. It was the task of the Southern Germanic peoples to develop first of all what pertains to the inward preparation of the Spiritual Soul, imbuing it with spiritual substance of the old clairvoyance, transposed now on to the physical plane.

The philosophies of Central Europe represented by Fichte,

Schelling and Hegel in the nineteenth century seem far removed from the sphere of mythology. Nevertheless they are simply the product of the highest sublimation of the old clairvoyant insight, of the cooperation of the divine-spiritual Beings within the heart of man. Otherwise it would not have been possible for a Hegel to have looked upon his ideas as realities; it would have been impossible for him to make the strange remark, so characteristic of the man, when, in answer to the question, "What is the abstract?" he replied: "The abstract is for instance an individual who fulfils his daily duties—the carpenter, for example." What is concrete to the purely abstract theorist was therefore abstract to Hegel. What to the purely abstract theorist are mere thoughts, were to him great, mighty architects of the world. Hegel's philosophy is the final, the most highly sublimated expression of the Spiritual Soul and embodies in the form of pure concepts that which Nordic man still saw as sensible-supersensible, divine-spiritual powers associated with the 'I'. The 'I' of Fichte's philosophy was simply the precipitation of what the God Thor had given to the human soul, only viewed from the standpoint of the Spiritual Soul and clothed seemingly in the barest of thoughts, the thought of "I am", which is the starting-point of Fichte's philosophy. From the gift of the 'I' by the God Thor or Donar to the ancient Nordic peoples from the spiritual world, down to this philosophy, evolution follows a straight line. Thor had to prepare this development for the Spiritual Soul in order that this Soul might have the content appropriate for its task which is to turn towards the external world and to work within that world. But this philosophy is aware not only of the external world of crude empiric experience, but finds in the external world the content of the Spiritual Soul itself and regards nature simply as the idea in its other aspect. The mission of the Nordic-Germanic peoples in Central Europe is to ensure that this impulse lives on.

Now since all evolution is a continuous process we must ask ourselves what form it takes. When we look back into ancient times we observe a remarkable phenomenon. We have already said that the first manifestations of ancient Indian culture were expressed through the etheric body after the spiritual forces of soul had been adequately developed. There are however other civilizations which have also preserved the old Atlantean culture and carried it over into the post-Atlantean epoch. Whilst, on the one hand, the ancient Indian was able to return to the etheric body with highly developed faculties of soul and out of the forces of this body created his great civilization and lofty spiritual life, we have, on the other hand, a culture which originated in Atlantis and continued to work on in the post-Atlantean epoch, a culture which owes its origin and development to its emphasis upon the other aspect of the consciousness of the etheric body. This is the Chinese culture. If you bear this connection in mind and remember that the Atlantean culture was directly related to what in our earlier lectures we called the "Great Spirit", you will understand the peculiarities of Chinese culture. This culture was directly connected with the highest stages of world-evolution. But it still works into the bodies of men today and from an entirely different angle. It seems very likely, therefore, that these two civilizations, the two great polarities of the post-Atlantean epoch, will clash at some future time—the Indian which, within certain limits, is capable of development, and the Chinese that isolates itself and remains static, repeating what existed in the old Atlantean epoch. One literally receives an occult, scientific, poetic impression if one follows the evolution of the Chinese Empire, if one thinks of the Great Wall of China which sought to exclude completely everything which originated in primeval times and had been developed in the post-Atlantean epoch. Something like an occult, poetic feeling steals over one if one compares the Wall of China with what had once existed in former times. I can give only the barest indications about these matters. If you compare them with the existing findings of science you will find how extraordinary illuminating they are. Let us consider clairvoyantly the old continent of Atlantis which will be found where the Atlantic Ocean now lies, between Africa and Europe on the one side and America on the other. This continent was encircled by a warm stream which, strange as it may seem, was seen clairvoyantly to flow from the South through Baffin Bay towards the North of Greenland, encircling it. Then, turning eastward, it gradually cooled down. Long before the continents of Russia and Siberia had emerged, it flowed past the Ural mountains, changed course, skirted the Eastern Carpathians, debouched into the region now occupied by the Sahara and finally reached the Atlantic Ocean in the neighbourhood of the Bay of Biscay. Thus it followed a strictly delimited course. Only the last remaining traces of this stream are still extant. This stream is the Gulf Stream which at that time encircled the Atlantean continent. Now you will recall that in their psychic life the Greeks experienced a memory of the spiritual worlds. The picture of Oceanus which is a memory of that Atlantean epoch arose within them. Their picture of the world, their cosmogony, was very near the truth because it was derived from the old Atlantean epoch. The stream that flowed southward via Spitzbergen as a warm current and gradually cooled, etc., followed a strictly delimited course. This circumscribed course was unmistakeably echoed in the Chinese culture, a culture circumscribed by the Great Wall and which had been brought over from Atlantis. The Atlantean civilization had as yet no history, hence the Chinese civilization also has preserved an element of the unhistorical. It preserves something of the pre-Indian culture, something surviving from old Atlantis.

Let us now describe the further progress of the Germanic and Nordic Folk Spirit. What consequences will ensue when a Folk Spirit so directs his people that the Spirit Self in particular can develop? Let us remember that the etheric body was developed in the ancient Indian epoch, the sentient body in the Persian, the Sentient Soul in the Egypto-Chaldean, the Intellectual Soul (or Mind-Soul) in the Graeco-Latin, the Spiritual Soul (or Consciousness-Soul) in our present epoch which is not yet concluded. The next epoch will see the invasion of the Spiritual Soul by the Spirit Self, so that the Spirit Self shall irradiate the Spiritual Soul. This is the task of the sixth post-Atlantean civilization and must be prepared for gradually. This civilization which must be pre-eminently a receptive one, for it must reverently await the influx of the Spirit Self into the Spiritual Soul, is being prepared by the peoples of Western Asia and their outposts in Eastern Europe, the Slavonic peoples. The latter with their Folk Souls were the outposts of the coming sixth post-Atlantean epoch for the very good reason that future contingencies must to a certain extent be prepared beforehand, must already be anticipated in order to prepare the ground for future development. It is extremely interesting to study these outposts of a Folk Soul who is preparing himself for future epochs. This accounts for the peculiar character of the Slavonic peoples who are our immediate Eastern neighbours. In the eyes of the Western European their whole culture gives the impression of being in a preparatory stage and in a curious way, through the medium of their outposts, they present that which in spirit is wholly different from any other mythology. We should give a false impression of these Eastern outposts as a future civilization if we were to compare them with the culture of the Western European peoples who enjoy a continuous, unbroken tradition which is still rooted in, and has its source in the old clairvoyance. The peculiarity attaching to the souls of these Eastern European peoples is reflected in the whole attitude they have always shown when the question of their relations to the higher worlds arose. In comparison with our 'mythology' in Western Europe with its individual deities, their (i.e. the Slavonic peoples) relation to the higher worlds is totally different. What this Slavonic 'mythology' presents to us as the direct outpouring of the inner being of the people may be compared to the anthroposophical conception of successive planes or worlds through which we prepare ourselves to understand a higher spiritual culture. We find in the East, for example, the following conception: the West has been moulded by the influence of successive and related cultures. In the East we find, in the first place, a distinct consciousness of a world of the Cosmic Father. Everything that is creatively active in air and fire, in all the elements in and above the Earth, is embodied in the concept of the Heavenly Father, in one seemingly great, all-embracing idea which is at the same time an all-embracing feeling. Just as we think of the Devachanic world as fructifying our Earth, so this Divine world, the world of the Father, draws nigh from the East, fructifying that which is experienced as the Mother, the Spirit of the Earth. We have no other expression and can think of no other way of picturing the whole Spirit of the Earth than in the fertilization of Mother Earth. Instead of individual deities we

have then two contrasting worlds. And confronting these two
worlds as a third world is that which we feel to be the Blessed
Child of these two worlds. This Blessed Child is not an individual
being, not an emotional feeling, but something that is the
creation of the Heavenly Father and the Earth Mother. The
relation of Devachan to the Earth is perceived in this way from
the spiritual world. The birth of new life, the coming of springtime, and that which grows and multiplies in the material body
is felt as something wholly spiritual; and that which grows and
multiplies in the soul is perceived as the world which at the same
time is felt to be the Blessed Child of the Heavenly Father and
the Earth Mother. Universal as these conceptions are, we find
them among the outposts of the Slavonic peoples who have
advanced westwards. In no Western European mythology is
this conception so universal. In the West we find clearly defined
deities; but they are not the same as those which we depict in
our spiritual cosmogony; these are more nearly represented by
the Heavenly Father, the Earth Mother and the Blessed Child
of the East. In the conception of the Blessed Child there is again
a world which permeates another world. It is a world that is
envisaged as a separate world because it is associated with the
physical sun and its light. The Slavonic element also recognizes
this Being—though different, of course, in conception and feeling
—which we have so often met with in Persian mythology; it
recognizes the Sun Being who sheds his blessings upon the other
three worlds, so that the destiny of man is woven into creation,
into the Earth, through the fertilization of the Earth Mother by
the Heavenly Father and through that which the Sun Spirit
weaves into both these worlds. A fifth world is that which
embraces everything spiritual. The Eastern European feels the
spiritual world underlying all the forces of nature and all animate
beings. We must think of this as a wholly different sentient
response, as associated more perhaps with the phenomena,
creations and beings of nature.

We must think of this Slavonic soul as being able to see
entities in natural phenomena, to see not only the physical and
sensory aspects, but also the astral and spiritual. Hence the
Slavonic soul conceived of a vast number of Beings in this

strange spiritual world which we can at best compare with the world of the Elves of Light. The spiritual world which is looked upon in Spiritual Science as the fifth world is approximately the world which dawns in the hearts and minds of the peoples of Eastern Europe. Whatever name we attach to it is of no importance; what is of importance are the subtle shades and gradations of feelings of the Slavonic peoples and that the concepts which characterize this fifth plane or spiritual world are to be found in Eastern Europe. In this frame of mind this world of Eastern Europe was preparing for that Spirit which is to pour the Spirit Self into man in anticipation of the epoch when the Spiritual Soul shall be uplifted to receive the Spirit Self in the sixth post-Atlantean age which is to succeed our own. We meet with this in a unique manner not only in the creations of the Folk Souls who are as I have just described them, but we find it remarkably anticipated in the diverse manifestations of Eastern Europe and its culture.

It is most interesting to observe how the Eastern European expresses his natural receptivity to pure Spirit by assimilating Western European culture with great devotion, thus looking forward prophetically to the time when he will be able to unite something even greater with his being. Hence also his limited interest in isolated aspects of this Western European culture. He absorbs what is offered him more in broad outlines, ignoring the details, because he is preparing himself to assimilate that which is to enter mankind as the Spirit Self. It is particularly interesting to see how, under this influence, it has been possible for Eastern Europe to develop a much more advanced conception of the Christ than Western Europe, except in those areas of the West where the conception of the Christ has been introduced by Spiritual Science. Amongst those who do not accept the teachings of Spiritual Science the most advanced conception of Christ is that of the Russian philosopher, Solovieff. His conception of Christ is such that it can only be understood by students of Spiritual Science because he lifts it to ever higher planes and reveals its infinite potentialities, showing that our understanding of Christ today is only a beginning, because the Christ Impulse has only been able to reveal to mankind a fraction of what it holds in store. But if we look at the conception of Christ as presented by Hegel, for example, we find that Hegel understood Him as only the most refined, the most sublimated Spiritual Soul could understand Him. But Solovieff's conception of Christ is very different. He fully recognizes the dual nature of this conception. He rejects the endless theological polemics which in reality rest upon deep misunderstandings, because ordinary conceptions are inadequate for an understanding of the dual nature of Christ, and because they fail to develop in us any realization that the two aspects, the Human and the Divine, must be clearly distinguished. The concept of Christ rests upon a clear realization of what took place when the Christ Spirit entered into the man Jesus of Nazareth who had already developed all the necessary attributes. We must first of all understand the two natures of Christ and the union of both at a higher stage. As long as we have not grasped this duality, we have not understood the Christ in all His fullness. Only that philosophical understanding can achieve this which foresees that man himself will participate in a culture in which his Spiritual Soul will be able to receive the Spirit Self, so that in the sixth epoch of civilization man will feel himself to be a duality in whom the higher nature will curb the lower.

Solovieff carries this duality into his conception of Christ and emphasizes that this conception can be meaningful only if one accepts the existence of a divine and human nature which can only be understood if one recognizes that their cooperation is a reality, that they form not an abstract, but an organic unity. Solovieff already recognizes that we must think of this Being as possessing two centres of will. If you accept the teachings of Spiritual Science concerning the true significance of the Christ Being in their original form which stemmed, not from an imaginary, but from a spiritually real Indian influence, you will then have to think of Christ as having developed in His three bodies the capacities of feeling, thinking and willing. It is a human feeling, thinking and willing into which the Divine feeling, thinking and willing descends. The European man will only assimilate this completely when he has risen to the sixth stage of civilization. This had been prophetically expressed in Solovieff's anticipatory conception of Christ which announces the dawn of a later civilization. This philosophy of Eastern Europe therefore reaches far beyond that of Hegel and Kant, and in the presence of this philosophy one suddenly senses the first stirrings of a later development. It is far in advance because this conception of Christ is felt to be a prophetic anticipation, the dawn of the sixth post-Atlantean civilization. Consequently the whole Christ Being, the whole significance of Christ occupies a central place in philosophy and thus becomes totally different from the Western European conceptions of it. The conception of Christ, in so far as it has been developed outside Spiritual Science and is conceived as a living substance, as a living spiritual entity which shall permeate all social life and social institutions— which is felt as a Personality in whose service man finds himself as 'man endowed with Spirit Self'—this Christ-Personality is portrayed in a wonderfully concrete manner in Solovieff's various expositions of St. John's Gospel and its opening words. Only if we stand upon the ground of Spiritual Science can we comprehend Solovieff's profound interpretation of the sentence, "In the Beginning was the Word or Logos", and how differently St. John's Gospel is understood by a philosophy which in a remarkable way anticipates the future.

If, on the one hand, Hegel's philosophy marks a high point, something that is born out of the Spiritual Soul as the highest philosophical achievement, this philosophy of Solovieff, on the other hand, provides the seed in the Spiritual Soul for the philosophy of the Spirit Self which will be incorporated in the sixth cultural epoch. There is perhaps no greater contrast than that eminently Christian conception of the State which hovers as a great ideal before Solovieff as a dream of the future, that Christian conception of the social State which takes everything implicit in that conception in order to present it as an offering to the instreaming Spirit Self, in order to hold it up as an ideal of the future to be Christianized by the powers of the future—there is indeed no greater contrast than this idea of Solovieff's of a Christian community in which the Christ conception lies wholly in the future and the Divine State of St. Augustine who accepts, it is true, the Christ idea, but whose Divine State is simply the

Roman State with Christ incorporated in the Roman idea of the State. What provides the knowledge for the emergent Christianity of the future is the decisive question. In Solovieff's State Christ is the blood which circulates in the body social, and the essential point is that the State is envisaged as a concrete personality so that it will act as a living spiritual entity, but at the same time will fulfil its mission with all the idiosyncracies of a personality. No other philosophy is so deeply permeated by the Christ idea— the Christ idea which is anticipated in Spiritual Science at a higher level—and yet at the same time has remained so long in the germinal stage. Everything that we find in the East, from the make-up of the people to its philosophy, appears to us as something which contains only the germinal beginning of a future evolution and which, therefore, had also to submit to the special education of the Time Spirit of ancient Greece, the guiding Spirit of exoteric Christianity who was entrusted with the mission of becoming later on the Time Spirit for Europe. The make-up of this people whose task will be to develop the seed of the sixth culture-epoch had from the very beginning to be not only educated, but nursed and nurtured by that Time Spirit. And so we can literally say—and here Father concept and Mother concept lose their dual aspect—that the make-up of the Russian people which is destined to evolve gradually into the Folk Soul, was not only educated, but was nursed and nurtured by that which, as we have seen, had been developed out of the old Greek Time Spirit and had then assumed externally another rank.

Thus the various missions are distributed between Western, Central, Northern and Eastern Europe. I wished to give you an indication of these various missions. On the basis of these indications I propose to add further observations and show what the Europe of the future will be like, a future that will ensure that we must form our ideals on the basis of such knowledge. I propose to show how, through this influence, the Germanic and Nordic Folk Spirit is gradually transformed into a Time Spirit.

LECTURE ELEVEN

Nerthus, Freyja and Gerda. Twilight of the Gods.
Vidar and the new Revelation of Christ.

In beginning this our last lecture I can assure you that much
still remains to be discussed and that in this course of lectures we
have touched only the fringe of this subject which covers a wide
field. I can only hope that it will not be the last time that we
shall speak together here on kindred subjects, and it must suffice
if I have introduced this subject with only the briefest indications, since detailed discussion at this present moment would
otherwise create further complications.

Like a golden thread running through the last few lectures was
the idea that Teutonic mythology contains something which, in
imaginative form, is connected in a remarkable way with the
knowledge derived from the spiritual research of our time. Now
this is also one of the reasons why we may hope that the Folk
Spirit, the Archangel, who directs and guides this country
(Norway) will imbue modern philosophy and modern spiritual
research with the capacities he has developed over the centuries
and that henceforth modern spiritual research will be fertilized
by uniting with the life-forces of the entire people.

The further we penetrate into the details of Teutonic mythology, the more we shall realize—and this applies to no other
mythology—how wonderfully the deepest occult truths are
expressed in the symbols of this mythology. Perhaps some of you
who have read my *Occult Science—an Outline*, or have heard other
lectures which I was able to give here will recall that once upon
a time in the course of Earth-evolution an event occurred which
we may describe as the descent of those human souls who, in
primeval times before the old Lemurian epoch, for very special
reasons rose to other planets, to Saturn, Jupiter, Mars, Venus
and Mercury, and that these souls in the late Lemurian epoch

and throughout the Atlantean epoch, after the hardening forces of the Moon had left the Earth, endeavoured to incarnate in human bodies whose capacities had gradually been developed and perfected under Earth conditions. These Saturn-, Jupiter-, Mars-, Venus-, and Mercury-souls then descended upon Earth and this descent can still be verified today in the Akashic Records. During the Atlantean epoch the air of Atlantis was permeated with watery mists and through these mists those on Earth beheld with the old Atlantean clairvoyance the descent of these souls out of the Cosmos. Whenever new beings descended from spiritual heights into the still soft, plastic and pliant bodies of that time, this was understood to be the external manifestation of souls descending out of the Cosmos, out of the atmosphere, out of planetary spheres, in order to incarnate in earthly bodies.

These earthly bodies were fructified by that which poured down from spiritual heights. The memory of this event has survived in the imaginative conceptions of Teutonic mythology and has persisted so long that it was still extant amongst the Southern Germanic peoples at the time when Tacitus wrote his "Germania". No-one will understand the account Tacitus gives of the Goddess Nerthus unless he realizes that this event actually took place.* He relates that the chariot of the Goddess Nerthus was driven over the waters. Later on this survived as a solemn ritual; formerly it had been a matter of actual vision. This Goddess offered the human bodies that were suitable to the human souls descending from the planetary spheres. That is the mystery underlying the Nerthus myth and it has survived in all that has come down to us in the older sagas and legends which give intimations of the birth of physical man. Njördr who is intimately related to the Goddess Nerthus is her masculine counterpart. He is said to represent the primeval memory of the descent of the psycho-spiritual beings who in olden time had risen to

*Chapter 40 of *Germania*. See also the lecture given by Rudolf Steiner in Basle, 12.xii.1916, entitled *Christmas at a Time of Grievous Destiny*. Lecture IV in *The Festivals and their Meaning*. Vol. I. *Christmas*. (Rudolf Steiner Press).

planetary heights and who, during the Atlantean epoch, had come back and incarnated in human bodies.

In my pamphlet, *The Occult Significance of Blood,* you can read how miscegenation and contact between different peoples have played a significant rôle at certain periods. Now not only the mixture of peoples and their interrelationships which led to the introduction of foreign blood, but also the psychic and spiritual development of the Folk Spirits have played a decisive part. The vision of that descent has been preserved in the greatest purity in those sagas which arose in former times in these Northern regions. Hence in the Sagas of the Vanir you can still find one of the oldest recollections of this descent. Especially here in the North, the Finnish tradition still preserves a living memory of this union of the soul-and-spirit which descended from planetary spheres with that which springs out of the body of the Earth and which Northern tradition knows as Riesenheim (Home of the Giants). That which developed out of the body of the Earth belongs to Riesenheim. We realize, therefore, that Nordic man was always aware of spiritual impulses, that he felt within his gradually evolving soul the workings of this old vision of the Gods which was still natural to man here when, in those ancient times, the watery mists of Atlantis still covered the region. Nordic man felt within him some spark of a God who was directly descended from those divine-spiritual Beings, those Archangels who directed the union of soul-and-spirit with the terrestrial and physical. People believed and felt that the God Freyr and his sister Freyja who were once upon a time specially favoured Gods of the North, had originally been those angelic Beings who had poured into the human soul all that this soul required in order to develop further upon the physical plane those old forces which they (the people) had received through their clairvoyant capacities. Within the physical world, the world limited to the external senses, Freyr was the continuer of all that had hitherto been received in a clairvoyant form. He was the living continuation of forces clairvoyantly received. He had therefore to unite with the physical-corporeal instruments existing in the human body itself for the use of these soul-forces, which then transmit to the physical plane what had been perceived in primeval clairvoyance. This is reflected in the marriage of Freyr with Gerda, the Giant's daughter. She is born out of the physical forces of earthly evolution itself. The descent of the divine-spiritual into the physical is still mirrored in these mythological symbols. The figure of Freyr portrays in a remarkable way how Freyr makes use of that which enables man to manifest on the physical plane that for which he has been prepared through his earlier clairvoyance. The name of his horse is Bluthuf, indicating that the blood is an essential factor in the development of the 'I'. A remarkable magic ship is placed at his disposal. It could span the sky or be folded up to fit into a tiny box. What is this magic ship? If Freyr is the power which transmits clairvoyant forces to the physical plane, then this magic ship is something peculiarly his own: it symbolizes the alternation of the soul in day and night. Just as the human soul during sleep and until the moment of waking spreads out over the Macrocosm, so too the magic ship spreads its sails and is then folded up again into the cerebral folds to be stowed away in that tiny box—the human skull. You will find all this portrayed in a wonderful way in the mythological figures of Teutonic mythology.

Those of you who probe more deeply into these matters will be gradually convinced that what has been implanted, 'injected' into the mind and soul of this Northern people by means of these symbols or pictures is no flight of fancy, but actually stems from the Mystery Schools. Thus in the guiding Archangel or Folk Spirit of the North, much of the old education through clairvoyant perception has survived, much of that which may unfold in a soul which, in the course of its development on the physical plane, is associated with clairvoyant development.

Although not apparent from the external point of view today, the Archangel of the Germanic North had within him this tendency, and thanks to this tendency he is particularly fitted to understand modern Spiritual Science and to transform it in the appropriate manner to satisfy the inherent potentialities of the people. You will therefore appreciate why I have said that the soul of the Germanic peoples in particular is best fitted to understand what I could only indicate briefly in the public lecture which I gave here on the Second Coming of Christ.

Spiritual research today shows us that after Kali Yuga has run its course (which lasted for 5,000 years, approximately from 3,100 B.C. to A.D. 1,899) new capacities will appear in the isolated few who are specially fitted to receive them. A time will come when individuals will be able, through the natural development of the new clairvoyance, to perceive something of what is announced only by Spiritual Science or spiritual research. We are told that in the course of the next centuries, increasing numbers of people will be found in whom the organs of the etheric body are so far developed that they will attain to clairvoyance, which today can only be acquired through training. How are we to account for this? What will be the nature of the etheric body in those few who develop clairvoyance? There will be some who will receive clairvoyant impressions, and I should like to describe to you a typical example. A man performs some act and at the same time feels himself impelled to observe something. A sort of dream vision arises in him which at first he does not understand. But if he has heard of Karma, of how world-events conform to law, he will then realize, little by little, that what he has seen is the karmic counterpart of his present deeds made visible in the etheric world. Thus the first elements of future capacities are gradually developed.

Those who are open to the stimulus of Spiritual Science will, from the middle of the twentieth century on, gradually experience a renewal of that which St. Paul saw in etheric clairvoyance as a mystery to come, the 'Mystery of the Living Christ'. There will be a new manifestation of Christ, a manifestation which must come when human capacities develop naturally to the point when the Christ can be seen in the world in which He has always been present since the Mystery of Golgotha and in which He can also be experienced by the Initiate. Mankind is gradually growing into that world in order to be able to perceive from the physical plane that which formerly could be perceived only in the Mystery Schools from the perspective of the higher planes.

Nevertheless, occult training is still a necessity. It always presents things in a different light to those who have not undergone occult training. But occult training will, by the transformation of the physical body, show the Mystery of the Living

Christ in a new way—as it will be able to be seen etherically from the perspective of the physical plane by a few isolated individuals at first, and later by increasing numbers of people in the course of the next three thousand years. The Living Christ perceived by St. Paul, the Christ who is to be found in the etheric world since the Mystery of Golgotha, will be seen by an ever-increasing number of people.

The manifestations of the Christ will be experienced by man at ever higher levels. That is the mystery of the evolution of Christ. At the time of the Mystery of Golgotha it was intended that man should comprehend everything from the perspective of the physical plane. It was therefore necessary that he should be able to see Christ on the physical plane, to receive tidings of Him and to bear witness to His dominion on that plane. But mankind is designed to progress and to develop higher powers. He who believes that the manifestation of Christ will be repeated in the form which was valid nineteen hundred years ago can have little understanding of the development of mankind. The manifestation of Christ took place on the physical plane because, at that time, the forces of man were adapted to the physical plane. But those forces will evolve, and in the course of the next three thousand years Christ will be increasingly understood by the more highly developed souls on Earth.

What I have just said is a truth which has long been communicated to a select few from within the esoteric schools and it is a truth that today must pervade the teachings of Spiritual Science in particular, because Spiritual Science is intended to be a preparation for that which is to come. Mankind is now ready for freedom and self-knowledge and it is highly probable that those who proclaim themselves to be the pioneers of the Christ-vision will be denounced as fools on account of their message to mankind. It is possible for mankind to sink still deeper into materialism and to spurn that which could become a most valuable revelation for mankind. Everything that may happen in the future is to a certain extent subject to man's volition; consequently he may miss what is intended for his salvation. It is extremely important to realize that Spiritual Science is a preparation for the new Christ-revelation.

Materialism holds a twofold danger. The one which probably stems from the traditions of the West, is that everything that the first pioneers of the new Christ-revelation will announce in the twentieth century from out of their own vision will be dismissed as a figment of the imagination, as the height of folly. Today materialism has invaded all spheres. It is not only ingrained in the West, but has also invaded the East. There, however, it assumes another form. One consequence of oriental materialism might well be that mankind will fail to recognize the higher aspects of the Christ-revelation. And then will follow what I have often spoken of here, and which I must repeat again and again, namely, that materialistic thinking will have a purely materialistic conception of the manifestation of Christ. It might well be that, under the influence of spiritual-scientific truths, people might venture to speak of a future manifestation of Christ and yet believe that He will appear in a physical body. The result would simply be another form of materialism, a continuation of what has already existed for centuries.

People have always exploited this false materialism. Indeed certain individuals declared themselves to be the new Messiah. The last well-known case occurred in the seventeenth century, when a man called Sabbatai Zevi of Smyrna announced that he was the new Messiah. He made a great stir. Not only those who lived in his immediate environment made pilgrimages to visit him, but also people from Hungary, Poland, Germany, France, Italy and North Africa. Everywhere Sabbatai Zevi was regarded as the physical incarnation of a Messiah. I do not propose to relate the human tragedy that befell the personality of Sabbatai. In the seventeenth century no great harm was done. At that time man was not really a free agent, although he could recognize intuitively—which was a kind of spiritual feeling—what was the truth. But in the twentieth century it would be a great misfortune if, under the pressure of materialism, the manifestation of Christ were to be taken in a materialistic sense, implying that one must look for His return in a physical body. This would only prove that mankind had not acquired any perception of, or insight into the real progress of human evolution towards a higher spirituality.

False Messiahs will inevitably appear and, thanks to the material-ism of our time, they will find popular favour like Sabbatai in the seventeenth century. It will be a severe test for those who have been prepared by Spiritual Science to recognize where the truth lies, to know whether the spiritual theories are really permeated by a living, spiritual feeling or whether they are only a disguised form of materialism. It will be a test of the further development of Spiritual Science whether Spiritual Science will develop a sufficient number of people who are able to understand that they must perceive the spirit in the spirit, that they must seek the new manifestation of Christ in the etheric world, or whether they will refuse to look beyond the physical plane and expect to see a manifestation of Christ in the physical body. Spiritual Science has yet to undergo this test. There is no doubt that nowhere has the ground been better prepared to recognize the truth on this very subject than in Scandinavia where the Northern mythology flourished.

The twilight of the Gods embraces a significant vision of the future, and I now come to a theme which I have already touched upon. I have already told you that in a folk community which has so recently left its clairvoyant past behind it, a clairvoyant sense is also developed in its guiding Folk Spirit in order that the new-found clairvoyance can again be understood. Now if a people experiences the new epoch with new human capacities in the region where Teutonic mythology flourished, then this people must realize that the old clairvoyance must assume a different form after man has undergone development on the physical plane. The old clairvoyance was temporarily silenced; man lost for a while the vision of the world of Odin and Thor, of Baldur and Hödur, of Freyr and Freyja. But this world will return again in an epoch when other forces meanwhile have been at work upon the human soul. When man gazes out into the new world with the new etheric clairvoyance he will realize that the forces of the old Gods no longer avail. If the old forces were to persist, then the counter-forces would range themselves against that force whose function in olden times was to develop man's capacities to a certain level. Odin and Thor will be visible again, but now in a new form. All the forces opposed to Odin and Thor, everything which has developed as a counter-force will once again be visible in a mighty tableau. But the human soul would not progress, it would not be able to resist injurious influences if it were subject solely to the forces known to the old clairvoyance. Once upon a time Thor endowed man with an ego. This ego has been developed on the physical plane, has evolved out of the Midgard Snake which Loki, the Luciferic power, has left behind in the astral body. That which Thor was once able to give and which the human soul transcends, is in conflict with that which proceeds from the Midgard Snake. This is depicted in Nordic mythology as the conflict between Thor and the Midgard Snake. They are evenly matched, neither can prevail. In the same way Odin wrestles with the Fenris Wolf and does not prevail.* Freyr who, for a time, moulded the human soul-forces, had to succumb to that which had been given from out of the Earth-forces themselves to the 'I', which meanwhile had been developed on the physical plane. Freyr was overcome by the flaming sword of Earth-born Surtur.

All these details which are set down in the Twilight of the Gods will find their counterpart in a new etheric vision which in reality points to the future. But the Fenris Wolf, symbol of the relics of the old clairvoyance, will live on in the future. There is a very deep truth concealed in the fact that the struggle between the Fenris Wolf and Odin still persists. There will be no greater danger than the tendency to cling to the old clairvoyance which has not been permeated with the new forces, a danger which might tempt man to remain content with the manifestations of the old astral clairvoyance of primeval times, such as the soul-pictures of the Fenris Wolf. It would again be a severe trial for the future prospects of Spiritual Science, if, perhaps in the domain of Spiritual Science itself, there should arise a tendency to all sorts of confused, chaotic clairvoyance, an inclination to value clairvoyance illuminated by reason and spiritual knowledge less highly than the old, chaotic clairvoyance which is denied this

*On the day of Ragnarok (the Twilight of the Gods) Odin is swallowed up by the Fenris Wolf. For the relation between Odin and the Fenris Wolf, see Appendix.

12—MOFS • •

prerogative. These dark and confusing relics of the old clair-voyance would wreck a terrible vengeance. Such clairvoyance cannot be challenged by that which itself stemmed from the old clairvoyant gift, but only by that which, during the period of Kali Yuga, has matured in a healthy way in order to give birth to a new clairvoyance. The power given by the old Arch-angel Odin, the old clairvoyant powers, cannot save man; something very different must supplant them. These future powers however, are known to Teutonic mythology; it is fully aware of their existence. It knows that the etheric form exists in which shall be embodied what we are now to see again—Christ in etheric form. He alone will succeed in banishing the dark and impure clairvoyant powers which would confuse mankind if Odin should not succeed in overcoming the Fenris Wolf which symbolizes the atavistic clairvoyance. Vidar who has been silent until now will overcome the Fenris Wolf. We learn of this too in the Twilight of the Gods.

Whoever recognizes the significance of Vidar and feels him in his soul, will find that in the twentieth century the power to see the Christ can be given to man again. Vidar who is part of the heritage of Northern and Central Europe will again be visible to man. He was held secret in the Mysteries and occult schools—the God who should await his future mission. Only vague intim-ations of his image have been given. This may be seen from the fact that a picture has been found in the vicinity of Cologne and no-one knows whom it represents. But it is clearly a likeness of Vidar.

Throughout the period of Kali Yuga were acquired the powers which shall enable the new men to see the new manifestations of Christ. Those who are called upon to interpret from the signs of the times what is to come are aware that the new spiritual investi-gation will re-establish the power of Vidar who will banish from the hearts and minds of men all the dark and confusing relics of the old clairvoyance and will awaken in the human soul the new clairvoyance that is gradually unfolding.

When the wondrous figure of Vidar shines forth to us out of the Twilight of the Gods we realize that Teutonic mythology gives promise of future hope. We feel ourselves to be inwardly related to the figure of Vidar, the deeper aspects of whose being we are now striving to understand. We hope that those forces which the Archangel of the Teutonic world can contribute to the evolution of modern times will be able to provide the core and living essence of Spiritual Science. One part only of the development of mankind and the spirit—one part of a greater whole—has been realized for the fifth post-Atlantean epoch; another part has yet to be accomplished. Those members of the Nordic peoples who feel within them the elemental and vital energies of a young people will best be able to contribute to this development. This will to some extent be implanted in the souls of men; but they themselves must be prepared to make a conscious effort. In the twentieth century one may fall by the wayside because man must to a certain extent have free choice in determining his goal which must not be pre-determined. It is therefore a question of having a proper understanding of the goal ahead. If, then, Spiritual Science reflects the knowledge of the Christ Being, and if we start from a true understanding of this Being whom we look for in the very core of the European peoples themselves, if we set our future hopes on this understanding, then we shall not be motivated by any kind of personal predilection or temperamental predisposition.

It has sometimes been said that the name we give to the greatest Being in the evolution of mankind is of no consequence. He who recognizes the Christ Being will not insist on retaining the name of Christ. If we understand the Christ Impulse in the right way we would never say: a Being plays a part in the evolution of mankind, in the life of the peoples of the West and the East and this Being must conform to man's predilections for a particular truth. Such an attitude is not compatible with the teachings of occultism. What is compatible with occult teachings is that the moment one recognizes that this Being should be given the name of Buddha, we should unhesitatingly abide by our decision irrespective of whether we agree with it or not. Fundamentally it is not a question of sympathy or antipathy, but of the factual truth.

The moment the facts are open to other interpretations we should be prepared to act differently. Facts and facts alone must decide. We have no wish to introduce Orientalism and Occidentalism into what we look upon as the life-blood of Spiritual Science; if we should discover in the realm of the Nordic and Germanic Archangels a source of potential nourishment for true Spiritual Science, then this will not be the prerogative of a particular people or tribe in the Germanic countries, but of the whole of humanity. What is given to all mankind must be given; it may, it is true, originate in a particular region, but it must be given to the whole of humanity. We do not differentiate between East and West. We accept with deep gratitude the surpassing grandeur of the primeval culture of the holy Rishis in its true form. We accept with gratitude the Persian culture, the Egypto-Chaldean and Graeco-Latin cultures, and with the same objectivity we also accept the cultural heritage of Europe. We are compelled by the needs of the situation to present the facts as they really are.

If we incorporate the total contributions which each religion has made to the civilizing process of mankind into what we recognize to be the common property of mankind, then the more we do this, the more we are acting in accordance with the Christ-principle. Since this principle is capable of further development we must abandon the dogmatic interpretation of the early centuries and millennia when the initial stages of the Christ-principle were only imperfectly understood. We do not look to the past for future guidance. We do not seek to perpetuate the Christ of the past; we are chiefly concerned with what can be investigated by means of spiritual perception. To us the essential element in the Christ-principle does not belong to the past—however much tradition may insist upon this—but to the future. We endeavour to ascertain what is to come. We do not rely so much on historical tradition which was fundamental to the Christ Impulse at the beginning of the Christian era; we do not attach much importance to the external and historical approach. After Christianity has passed through its growing pains, it will develop further. It has gone forth into foreign lands and sought to convert the people to the particular Christian dogmas of the age. But we profess a Christianity which proclaims that Christ was active in all ages and that we shall find Him wheresoever we go, that the Christ-principle is the highest expression of Anthroposophy. And if Buddhism acknowledges as Buddhists only those who swear by Buddha, then Christianity will be the faith that swears by no prophet because it is not subject to a religious Founder attached to a particular people, but recognizes the God of all mankind.

Every Christian knows that the focal point of Christianity is a Mystery which became manifest on the physical plane at Golgotha. It is the perception of this Mystery which leads to the new vision I have described. We may also be aware that the spiritual life at the time of the Mystery of Golgotha was such that the Mystery could only be experienced in the form it was experienced at that time. We refuse to submit to dogmas, even those of a Christian past. If a dogma should be imposed upon us, irrespective of its source, we would reject it in the name of the true Christ-principle. However many may try to force the historical Christ into the Procrustean bed of a confessional creed, however many may declare that our vision of the future Christ is mistaken, we shall not allow ourselves to be led astray when they declare that He must be after this or that fashion, even when it comes from the lips of those who ought to know who Christ is. Equally, the idea of the Christ Being should not be limited or circumscribed by Eastern traditions, nor be coloured by the dogmas of Oriental dogmatism. What is taught out of the true sources of occultism concerning the evolution of the future must be free and independent of all tradition and authority.

It is a source of wonder to me how much agreement there is amongst the people assembled here. Those, not of Norse extraction, who have come here, have repeatedly said to me in the last few days how free they feel in their relations with the people of the Scandinavian North. It is proof, if proof were needed, that we are able, though some may not be conscious of it, to understand each other at the deepest levels of spiritual knowledge and that we shall understand each other, especially in those matters I emphasized at the last Theosophical Congress in Budapest and which I repeated during our own General Meeting in Berlin when we had the great pleasure of seeing friends from Norway amongst us. It would be disastrous for Spiritual Science if he who cannot yet see into the spiritual world were obliged to accept in blind faith what he is told. I beg of you now, as I begged of you in Berlin, never to accept on authority or on faith anything I have said or shall say. Even before one has reached the stage of clairvoyance it is possible to test the results of clairvoyant vision. I beg of you not to accept as an article of faith whatever I have said about Zarathustra and Jesus of Nazareth, about Hermes and Moses, Odin and Thor, and about Christ Jesus Himself, nor to accept my statements as authoritative. I beseech you to abjure the principle of authority, for that principle would be deleterious to our Movement.

I am sure, however, that when you begin to reflect objectively, when you say, "We have been told so and so; let us investigate the records accessible to us, the religious and mythological documents, let us check the statements of the natural scientists", you will realize how right I am. Avail yourselves of every means at your disposal, the more the better. I have no qualms. All that is given out of Rosicrucian sources can be tested in every way. Armed with the most materialistic criticism of the Gospels, verify what I have said about Christ Jesus, verify it as thoroughly as possible by all the means at your command on the physical plane. I am convinced that the more thoroughly you test it, the more you will find that what has been given out of the sources of the Rosicrucian Mystery will correspond to the truth.

I take it for granted that the communications given out from Rosicrucian sources will be tested rather than believed, tested not superficially by the superficial methods of modern science, but ever more conscientiously. Take the latest achievements of natural science with its most recent techniques, take the results of historical and religious research, it is all one to me. The more you test them, the more you will find them confirmed from this source. You must accept nothing on authority. The best students of Spiritual Science are those who take what is said as a stimulus in the first place and test it by the facts of life itself. For in life too, at every stage of life, you can test what is given out from the sources of Rosicrucianism. It is far from my intention in these lectures to lay down dogmas and claim that the facts are such and such and must be believed. Verify them by an exchange of views with people of able and active mind and you will find confirmation of what has been said as a prophetic indication of the future manifestation of Christ. You need only open your eyes and verify it objectively; we make no appeal to belief in authority. This need to test everything received from Spiritual Science should become a kind of basic attitude permeating our whole approach.

I should like to impress upon you, therefore, that it is not anthroposophical to accept a statement as dogma on the authority of this or that person; but it is truly anthroposophical to allow oneself to be stimulated by Spiritual Science and to verify what is communicated by life itself. Then, whatever might colour in any way a truly anthroposophical view will cease to exist. Neither Eastern nor Western predilections must be allowed to colour our view. He who speaks from the point of view of Rosicrucianism accepts neither Orientalism nor Occidentalism; both appeal to him equally. The inner nature of the facts alone determine their truth. He must bear this in mind, especially at such an important moment as this when we have indicated the Folk Spirit who rules over the Northern lands. Here dwells the Teutonic mythological Spirit; even though his presence is not felt, his influence is more widely diffused in Europe than one imagines. If a conflict were to arise between the peoples of the North it could not arise because one people disputed the contributions to the common weal. Each people must practise self-knowledge and ask itself: how can I best contribute to the common weal? Then, that which leads to the collective progress of all, to the common welfare of mankind, will be harvested. The sources of what we are able to contribute lie in our individual characteristics. The Teutonic Archangel will bring to the whole field of culture in the future what he is most fitted for in accordance with the capacities he has acquired which we have already outlined. By virtue of this inherent power he is able to ensure that what could not yet be presented in the first half of the fifth post-Atlantean epoch may play its part in the second half, namely, that spiritual element which we were able to recognize in a germinal, prophetic form in the Slav philosophy and in the national sentiment of the Slavonic peoples. This preparatory stage lasted for the first half of the fifth post-Atlantean age. At first, all that could be achieved by way of philosophy was a highly sublimated spiritual perception. This must then be grasped and permeated by the vital energies of the people so that it may become the common property of all mankind and may be realized in all aspects of our earthly life. Let us try to come to an understanding on this subject, for then this somewhat dangerous theme will have caused no great harm if all who are assembled here from the North, South, East, West and Centre of Europe feel that this theme is really important for the whole of humanity, that the larger nations no less than the smaller isolated groups have each their appointed mission and have to contribute their share to the whole. Often the smallest national fragments have most important contributions to make because it is given to them to preserve and nurture old and new motifs in the soul-life. Thus, even though we have made this dangerous topic the subject of our lectures, it will serve to foster the basic sentiment of a community of soul amongst all those who are united under the banner of Anthroposophical thought and feeling and of Anthroposophical ideals.

Only if we should still react out of sympathy and antipathy, if we have no clear understanding of the essence of our Anthroposophical Movement, could misunderstandings arise from what has been said. But if we have grasped the underlying spirit of these lectures, then the ideas presented may also help us to make the firm resolution to harbour the high ideal—each from his own standpoint and from his own background—to contribute to the common goal that which is inherent in our mission. We can best achieve this through our individual initiative and our natural predisposition. We can best serve mankind if we develop our particular talents so as to offer them to the whole of humanity as a sacrifice which we bring to the progressive development of culture. We must learn to understand this. We must learn to understand that it would not redound to the credit of Spiritual Science, if it did not contribute to the evolution of man, Angel and Archangel, but were to support the convictions of one people at the expense of another. It is no part of Spiritual Science to assist in imposing the confessional beliefs of one continent upon another continent. If the religious teachings of the East were to prevail in the West, or vice versa, that would be a complete denial of Anthroposophical teaching. What alone accords with Anthroposophical teaching is that we should unselfishly dedicate the best that is in us, our sympathy and compassion, to the well-being of all mankind. And if we are self-contained, and live, not for ourselves but for all men, then that is true Anthroposophical tolerance. I had to add these words by way of explanation for this somewhat delicate subject might otherwise offend national susceptibilities.

Spiritual Science, as we shall realize more and more clearly, will bring an end to the divisions of mankind. Therefore now is the right moment to learn to know the Folk Souls, because the province of Spiritual Science is not to promote antagonism between them, but to call upon them to work in harmonious cooperation. The better we understand this, the better students of Spiritual Science we shall be. On this note we shall end for the time being the course of lectures given here. For the knowledge we gather must ultimately find an echo in our feelings and our thinking and in the Anthroposophical goal we set before us. The more we practise this in our lives, the better Anthroposophists we are.

I have found that many of those who have accompanied us to Oslo have received a most favourable impression which they hasten to express in the words, "how much at home we feel here in the North!" And if higher spiritual forces are to be awakened in mankind, which we shall certainly see realized in the future, then to use the words of Vidar, the Aesir who has been silent until now, he will become the active friend of cooperative work, of cooperative endeavour, for which purpose we have all assembled here. With this object in view let us take leave of one another after having been together for a few days, and let us always remain together in spirit with this intention. Irrespective of where we students of Spiritual Science come from, whether from near or far, may we always meet together in harmony, even when we discuss amongst ourselves the particular characteristics of the peoples inhabiting the various countries of the Earth. We know that these are only the several tongues of flame which will mount together into the mighty flame upon the altar—the united progress of mankind—through the Anthroposophical view of life which lies so close to our hearts and is so deeply rooted in our souls.

(See Lectures Eight and Eleven)

Odin

Odin's sacrifice of higher rank becomes transformed into a higher power—he becomes lord of the runes, the creator of language. In the language of the Mysteries this renunciation is described as the sacrifice of Odin's eye at the fount of Mimir. This eye is the clairvoyant eye which, as pineal gland, lost its function in the course of evolution. At the same time this sacrifice prepares the development of independence and freedom, for only by serving his intimate relationship with the Gods is man able to stand four-square upon the Earth and become self-reliant.

Odin and the Fenris Wolf

(*a*) The prose Edda recounts the destiny of the three children of Loki: the Midgard Snake, the Fenris Wolf and Hel. Odin flung the Midgard Snake into the ocean, consigned Hel to Niflheim and kept the Fenris Wolf to himself. At the Twilight of the Gods the Wolf was destined ultimately to destroy him. The Ahrimanic forces which feed upon the living substance of the etheric body are portrayed in the figure of the Fenris Wolf. And because it threatened danger to the Aesir they bound it with a silken ribbon to a rock. (They were unwilling to kill the Wolf in order to avoid polluting the sanctuary with blood.)

(*b*) The original language of Atlantis was a unity. It was the creation of Odin with the formative forces of the laryngeal organism. Through the alliance of Odin and Loki, Ahrimanic forces entered into the etheric body and the organism of speech. The power of Ahriman (present in the undivided, primal language of Atlantis) perished after the Atlantean catastrophe— this is the Fenris Wolf of Nordic tradition. Wherever human speech or language becomes a means of concealing the spiritual world or denying its reality, we find the influence of the Fenris Wolf. Where the word describes only sensible phenomena or physical facts to the exclusion of supersensible or spiritual facts, Odin has succumbed to the Fenris Wolf. Ahrimanic influences gradually blunt the response of the etheric body. It loses its former receptivity to life processes: this is reflected in the shifting of consonants in the Indo-European languages (Grimm's Law). On the one hand, new elements are added, on the other, articulation becomes more indefinite, more insensitive; symptoms of paralysis set in—amalgamations, loss or disappearance of certain vowels and consonants. The original language which was a unity is split up into diverse tongues, into dialects. Here is seen the influence of the Fenris Wolf. Through the Fenris Wolf death enters into the organism of language—dead languages, e.g. Latin, have therefore become victims of the Fenris Wolf.

Odin and Thor

Thor is the son of Odin. Whilst the power of Odin is present in respiration and language, Thor works in the blood, in the rhythmic pulse-beat. Blood is the physical expression of the ego in the metabolic system. Thor is portrayed in the sagas as a choleric with red blood, quick to anger, ever ready to wield his hammer Mjölnir and endowed with a powerful will. Odin's sphere of activity is the astral body, that of Thor the etheric body.

The alliterative verse of Old Norse (the poetic Edda), Old English (Beowulf), Old Saxon (Heliand) and Old High German (Hildebrandslied) is based on two rhythmic laws—the rhythm of respiration and the rhythm of blood. A single breath corresponds to four pulse beats (eighteen and seventy-two to the minute respectively). This ratio of 1 : 4 is found in the long line which consisted of two half verses separated by a caesura. Each hemistich had two strongly accented syllables. Thus in the form and law of alliterative verse is reflected the relationship of Odin and Thor. The Völuspa was written in this metre known as Fornyrthislag.

This whole subject is treated in detail in Chapters IX and X of Ernst Uehli's *Nordisch-Germanische Mythologie als Mysteriengeschichte* (Rudolf Geering Verlag, Basel 1926) to which I am indebted for many of the above suggestions.

LIST OF RELEVANT LITERATURE

List of literature.
By Rudolf Steiner:
    Occult Science—an Outline (1962/3 edition)
    Theosophy
    Cosmic Memory: Prehistory of Earth and Man
    Knowledge of the Higher Worlds. How is it achieved?
    Christianity as mystical Fact

Lecture Courses:
    Genesis: Secrets of the Bible Story of Creation (10 lectures)
    True and False Paths in Spiritual Investigation (11 lectures)
    Inner Realities of Evolution (5 lectures)
    Spiritual Hierarchies and their Reflection in the physical World
       (10 lectures)
    Supersensible Influences in the History of Mankind (6 lectures)
    Wonders of the World, Ordeals of the Soul, Revelations of the Spirit
       (10 lectures)
    Man in the light of Occultism, Theosophy and Philosophy (10 lectures)
    Man as Symphony of the Creative Word (10 lectures)
    Occult History: Personalities and Events in World History in the light
       of Spiritual Science (6 lectures)
    Macrocosm and Microcosm (11 lectures)
    World History in the light of Anthroposophy (8 lectures)
    The True Nature of the Second Coming (2 lectures)